CREEDS AND CONFESSIONS

THE REFORMATION AND ITS MODERN ECUMENICAL IMPLICATIONS

DUCKWORTH

Studies in Theology

ATKINSON LEE. Groundwork of the Philosophy of Religion.

THEODORE H. ROBINSON. The Poetry of the Old Testament.
Prophecy and the Prophets in Ancient Israel.
A Short Comparative History of Religions.

H. WHEELER ROBINSON. Religious Ideas of the Old Testament.
The History of Israel.

J. K. MOZLEY. The Doctrine of the Atonement.

SYDNEY CAVE. An Introduction to the Study of Some Living
Religions of the East.
Christianity and Some Living Religions of the East.
The Christian Estimate of Man.
The Doctrine of the Person of Christ.

H. A. A. KENNEDY. The Theology of the Epistles.

E. BASIL REDLICH. Form Criticism.

W. R. INGE. Faith and its Psychology.

W. F. HOWARD. Christianity according to St. John.

A. S. PEAKE. Christianity : Its Nature and Truth.

A. DAKIN. Calvinism.

ROBERT S. FRANKS. The Doctrine of the Trinity.

SIR FREDERIC KENYON. The Text of the Greek Bible.

ALEXANDER SOUTER and C. S. C. WILLIAMS. The Text and Canon
of the New Testament.

G. B. CAIRD. The Apostolic Age.

JAMES D. WOOD. The Interpretation of the Bible.

G. W. ANDERSON. A Critical Introduction to the Old Testament.

G. ERNEST WRIGHT. An Introduction to Biblical Archæology.

F. L. CROSS. The Early Christian Fathers.

L. H. BROCKINGTON. A Critical Introduction to the Apocrypha.

CREEDS AND CONFESSIONS

The Reformation and its Modern Ecumenical Implications

by

ERIK ROUTLEY

(Minister of Augustine-Bristo Congregational Church, Edinburgh. Formerly Mackennal Lecturer in Ecclesiastical History at Mansfield College, Oxford)

GERALD DUCKWORTH & CO. LTD.
3 Henrietta Street, London, W.C. 2

First Published 1962

© 1962 by ERIK R. ROUTLEY

Printed in Great Britain
by T. and A. CONSTABLE LTD., Hopetoun Street,
Printers to the University of Edinburgh

PREFACE

THE object of this book is to introduce the reader to the classic Confessions of the Reformed Churches, and to provide for him the ground on which he may judge the process of inter-church relations in the days of the Reformation; and thereafter to show how the ecumenical movement of today has modified and criticized the approach to church relations implied in the Confessions. I have thought it best to allow the Confessions to speak for themselves (through my own précis and abridgement, provided to save time and space) and to leave detailed theological comment to those points which especially demand it, or to the sources in which the reader may readily find it.

I offer my warmest thanks to the Editor of this series (Dr. Nathaniel Micklem) for inviting me to make this contribution, and to the Librarians of Mansfield College, Oxford, and the Scottish Congregational College, Edinburgh, for a good deal of help.

E. R.

Edinburgh, 1961

CONTENTS

ABBREVIATIONS

In order to save space, the classic Confessions are often referred to in the following text by italic initials. The key to these is as follows:

A Augsburg Confession

T Council of Trent

FC Formula of Concord

1H, 2H First, Second Helvetic Confession

F French Confession (Gallican)

B Belgic Confession

W Westminster Confession

S Savoy Declaration

I.—INTRODUCTION

CREED AND CONFESSION

The greater part of this book is concerned with the Confessions of the Reformed Churches of the sixteenth and seventeenth centuries, together with some account of the decrees of Trent and the Articles of the Church of England. Its last chapter, by way of epilogue, is concerned with certain modern movements towards Church unity, and will be found to have very little to say of Confessions.

The Confession is a kind of ecclesiastical literature which may well now be judged to have passed into history and to be characteristic of a quite short period of history (roughly 1530-1700). The Confession bears relation to an older kind of document, the Creed; but it is not a Creed. The difference ought to be observed at once.

Creeds grew up in the Church of the first five centuries[1] as a natural fulfilment of a natural need—the need of objectifying experience. If experience, which is essentially a function of the individual, is to be changed into something which can be shared by others and transmitted from generation to generation, the change through which it must pass is objectification, and the new form it takes will be a tradition.

A tradition is that which is 'handed on' or 'handed over'. The word (as G. L. Prestige memorably wrote[2]) contains a strange counterpoint of meanings. *Tradere* means 'to hand over', but also 'to betray'. The word *tradition* contains not only the note of responsibility but also that of risk—the risk which death obliges us all to take. That which is precious enough to deserve preservation for our posterity we must 'hand on', taking always the risk that posterity will abuse it when we

---

[1] See J. N. D. Kelly, *Early Christian Creeds* (1950), esp. chapters II and III.

[2] G. L. Prestige, *Fathers and Heretics* (1940), chapter I.

THE APOSTLES' CREED

I believe in God the Father Almighty, Maker of heaven and earth: and in Jesus Christ his only Son our Lord, Who was conceived by the Holy Ghost, Born of the Virgin Mary, Suffered under Pontius Pilate, Was crucified, dead and buried, He descended into hell; The third day he rose again from the dead, He ascended into heaven, And sitteth on the right hand of God the Father Almighty; From thence he shall come to judge the quick and the dead.

I believe in the Holy Ghost; the holy Catholic Church; the Communion of Saints; the Forgiveness of sins; the Resurrection of the body; And the Life everlasting. Amen.

(This is the English Book of Common Prayer's translation of the received text of the Apostles' Creed. To give a date to the original document is virtually impossible. A document very like this is the subject of the Commentary of Rufinus (A.D. 404), and Rufinus says that he is setting it down as it was agreed by the Apostles after Pentecost and before they began systematically to preach the Gospel. This is no doubt rightly judged a 'pious fiction' (as in J. N. D. Kelly, *Early Christian Creeds*, 1950, p. 4). While in its present form the document may be quite late, it is essentially an expansion of the baptismal creed found in the Apostolic Constitutions of Hippolytus (early third century); and it may safely be regarded, as C. H. Dodd has said in his *The Apostolic Faith*, as a not unsatisfactory summary of the Apostles' teaching.)

THE NICENE CREED

I believe in one God the Father Almighty, Maker of heaven and earth, And of all things visible and invisible:

And in one Lord Jesus Christ, the only begotten Son of God, Begotten of his Father before all worlds, God of God, Light of Light, Very God of very God, Begotten, not made, Being of one substance with the Father, by whom all things were made: Who for us men, and for our salvation came down from heaven, And was incarnate by the Holy Ghost of the Virgin Mary, And was made man. And was crucified also for us under Pontius Pilate. He suffered and was buried, And the third day he rose again according to the Scriptures, And ascended into heaven, And sitteth on the right hand of the Father. And he shall come again with glory to judge both the quick and the dead: Whose kingdom shall have no end.

And I believe in the Holy Ghost, The Lord and giver of life, Who proceedeth from the Father and the Son, Who with the Father and the Son together is worshipped and glorified, Who spake by the prophets. And I believe one Catholic and Apostolic Church. I acknowledge one Baptism for the remission of sins. And I look for the Resurrection of the dead, And the life of the world to come. Amen.

(This is the English Book of Common Prayer's translation of the Creed published in 381 by the Council of Constantinople, with the modifications of the Council of Toledo, 589. It is based on, but importantly differs from, the creed presented at the Council of Nicaea, 325).

have gone. The provision against this risk is the process of objectification.

In the process of handing on the Faith from one generation to the next, two actions at least are required: that the elder shall teach the younger, and that the younger shall show evidence that he has understood and made his own what he has been taught. Faithful teaching demands as response not merely assent, but the sight of a new growth; teaching the faith is not putting a suit of clothes on a young man, but grafting a living tissue into him. Therefore the earliest creeds are intimately associated with baptism and with the catechism (teaching by question and answer) that goes before it. The credal formula is first the basis of teaching, and second the substance of what the candidate at baptism declares to be his own faith.

These are the conclusions to which the historians are led by such evidences of primitive creeds as is available to us. What we now know as the 'Nicene' and 'Apostles'' Creeds (dating respectively from, broadly, the year 381 and some unspecified date in the early period) are formalized, ecumenical versions of what had begun by being local scripture-derived formulae. They are the end-products of a process by which creeds had added to their function of unifying the generations, a function also of unifying the visible Church, the horizontal, as it were, was added to the vertical.

But as soon as it was accepted that creeds should be gestures of unity, it became also accepted that they should be tests of orthodoxy. A Creed became then not only 'what Christians all believe', but 'what any must believe if he is to call himself a Christian'. And the claim to orthodoxy inevitably generates controversy between those to whom orthodoxy is welcome or natural and those who seek to test it with questions or even dissents. In consequence, in the classic ecumenical creeds there is also an element of polemic, which expresses itself in rhetoric.

These, then, are the five components in the evolution of creeds:

(1) The basis of catechesis.

(2) The declaration of the candidate at baptism.

(3) The means of unifying the visible Church.

(4) The test of orthodoxy.

(5) The denunciation of heresy.

In what we know as the 'Nicene' Creed (which was, but for two small changes, the product not of the Council of Nicaea, 325, but of that of Constantinople, 381) we can discern all these elements: the scriptural basis for teaching (most evident in the section which deals with the birth, death, resurrection and ascension of Christ); the personal declaration—'I believe'; the means of unity and the test of orthodoxy (not in its text, but in its historical context, and especially in the use made of it by Theodosius); the polemic, in 'God of God, Light of Light, Very God of very God, Begotten, not made, Being of one substance with the Father'.

The 'Nicene' Creed and the two councils with which it is associated are described as 'ecumenical' because their open purpose was to treat the visible Church as a single body. It was not so much to unify it as to treat it as a unity. Unity in the Church had already, by 325, been the subject of discussion and even dispute. Schism has its roots in the Apostolic age itself ('I am of Paul; I am of Apollos', 1 Cor. i. 12). Cyprian delivered himself of a treatise of historic value on the subject in *De Unitate*, in which he showed that it was at bottom lack of charity, issuing in theological bitterness, which divided the Church. The Novatian schism which was the occasion of that treatise, and the later Donatist schism, had shown how precarious was the unity of the Church even during the pre-Constantinian age, and the publication of the first creed of Nicaea in 325 proved to be the signal for furious controversy and the deepening of cleavages before its 'ecumenical' form was codified in 381. The Theodosian gesture of compulsory unity[1] initiated the notion of an 'established' orthodoxy, but its legalism prevented its being a significant operation in the cause of true Christian unity.

[1] See N. Q. King, *The Emperor Theodosius and the Establishment of Christianity* (1961), for a full and well-documented account of Theodosius, which shows how this generalization needs to be modified in closer study.

Creeds, then, hold unity and disunity in their texts. Our final chapter will show how in our day, more than in any previous age, the 'Nicene' and 'Apostles'' Creeds are a principle of Christian unity; but it can be judged, on the evidences of the intervening chapters, that in the age of the Confessions they were hardly less so. The unifying influence of the Creeds, so far as it went, was recognized throughout the period of the Reformation in the Western Churches, Protestant and Catholic, far more widely than it was recognized in the days when they were published. Whatever may have been their shortcomings and failures at the time, the Creeds have given proof of considerable staying-power under theological stress.

Confessions are not creeds. They presuppose creeds, and often they elaborate the beliefs set out in the creeds; but themselves they are manifestos, sometimes in the form of extended theological treatises, sometimes in the form of polemical statements. They differ from creeds chiefly in being characteristic of an age in which the unity of the visible church was precisely not the primary assumption. A Confession becomes the manifesto of a communion which wishes to make clear its difference from another, or from all others. It is not the founding principle of a Dissent, but the objectifying (with a greater or less degree of self-deception) of that Dissent. To understand the background of the Confessions, then, it is necessary to understand the origin and nature of that multiple Dissent against the One Holy Catholic Church, and the idea of such a Church, which after many generations of preparation made itself evident in the sixteenth century. It is also necessary to understand that the Confessions are designed to steer a middle course between that Roman Catholic system which the Reformers repudiated in their consciences and the extreme forms of Dissent which, as they saw them, threatened to reduce the Church to anarchy.

THE ANABAPTIST REFORMATION

There can be no doubt that the chief clue to this multiple Dissent which produced the Reformation is in Anabaptism.

Anabaptism, with its astonishing local proliferations, its conception of the martyr Church, its eloquent and fierce denunciations of all establishments, never itself became an establishment. It was, and essentially remains in its modern manifestations, pure Dissent. And it at once becomes relevant, because the first of the Confessions, that of Augsburg, is full of detailed denunciations of its tenets and practices.

Anabaptist origins are extremely obscure, and much of the history of their movement must be gathered from incidental records in town chronicles. In any case we must not here pursue it in detail.[1] It is clear that they derived their essential Dissent from those anti-clerical and anti-aristocratic groups who formed themselves during the later Middle Ages into groups for mutual edification and mild protest against the Establishment, and were collectively known as *Brethren*. They are related to the Lollard-like Continental movements which expressed in many different ways, but always with an emphasis on Bible study and personal piety, dissatisfaction with Catholicism. It is recorded that about the time when Luther made his first protest in the *Ninety-Five Theses* (1517), Anabaptist groups were operating in Basel (1514), Zürich (1515) and Mainz (1518)—and these are merely incidental records of operations which were no doubt to be found elsewhere as well.

There is no single word, or single phrase, which properly sums up Anabaptism. In a sense it was characterized by an intense individualism: yet the Anabaptists of Münster in the 1530s openly practised communism among themselves. Generally Anabaptism practised a near-fundamentalist piety; but, on the other hand, one stream of Anabaptism was strongly humanist and rationalist, and gave rise to the movement of Polish Unitarianism under the Socinus family.[2] They were normally apostles of the technique of passive resistance, but,

---

[1] See T. M. Lindsay, *History of the Reformation* (Edinburgh 1907), II, pp. 430-469, for what is still an extremely serviceable account of Anabaptism; and G. H. Williams (ed.), *Spiritual and Anabaptist Writers* (S.C.M., Library of Christian Classics, vol. XXV, 1957), for selections from their writings.

[2] Williams, *op. cit.*, p. 23 f.

under persecution, they fought for their lives, and their
doctrines were not infrequently extremely polemical. They
were active here, contemplative there. The nearest thing to a
compendious phrase describing Anabaptism is George
Williams's 'radical Reformation'. They were, in whatever
society they found themselves, the arch-protesters.

For all Luther's loathing of them, it was people of this sort
(working quietly before his time, but working openly and
protestingly and violently in many places during the years of
the Reformation) who prepared public opinion to receive his
teachings. Anabaptism was the expression of a radical protest
against the dilution of pure religion. That too was Luther's
protest. If Anabaptism became wild and hysterical at Münster,
if it was always disorganized and has remained intractable to
historical generalization, this was because it carried individualism in religion to its logical conclusion. Anabaptism was less
interested in 'unity' than any religious movement of any
consequence has ever been. But it broke through the crust of
popular resignation and ploughed up the ground into which
the Reformers could sow the evangelical seed.

What it is necessary to note here is that Anabaptism was
hated by all the orthodox Reformers because it appeared to be
the very incarnation of church disorder. It was not enough for
Luther, Melanchthon or Calvin to preach a Reformation which
(like one branch of Anabaptism) required a return to primitive
Biblical simplicity in church order and piety, or (like another)
called a faithful remnant out of the wicked world to wait for
the coming of the Kingdom of God.[1] It was against all their
principles to promote social revolution; politically they were
far from leftist, whatever their theology. It was contrary to all
their plans to promote the doctrine that the world was wholly
evil and that no Christian could hold civil office and keep his
faith. It was characteristic of all those Reformed communions
which gathered round the sixteenth century Confessions that
they sought to promote unity and order within their own
bounds, and did not shrink from imposing a discipline on their

[1] Williams, *op. cit.*, p. 22.

members which differed not at all in severity from that imposed
by the Catholic Church on the faithful, but which they justified
by appeal to the Bible, rejecting what was based on appeal
to tradition. The Reformers sought to reform the whole Church,
and in that sense sought unity; but in the interim period before
their dream came true they were bound to promote disunity.
The unity they sought, however, was bound up with the
obligation on Christians of living in the world, and not cutting
themselves off from it. They sought a Christian society, and
did not believe this to involve, as the Anabaptists believed, an
internal contradiction. The Reformers saw 'a Church' and 'a
Christian state' as not only a possibility but the will of God.
Anabaptism would not look at church order, and regarded a
Christian state as an absurdity.

But the protest of the orthodox Protestants, characteristic
as it was of a protest led by learned university men (Zwingli
always excepted: he is an exception to everything one says in
generalization about the Reformers), appeared to Anabaptists
as a feeble compromise, and Anabaptism seemed to the
Reformers a troublesome revolutionary cult which alienated
the sympathy of the powerful. History insists, however, that
those who heard the Reformers gladly included in the rank and
file very many who would have made nonsense of them but for
the radical change in the climate of opinion which Anabaptism
had produced.

Believers' baptism, which was part of the practice common
to all, or nearly all, Anabaptists, must be regarded at that stage
as being a clear claim associated with the claim of conscious
individual faith. Those who promoted it (finding much in
Scripture to confirm them) represented infant baptism as a
piece of trickery characteristic of a despotic Church. Not only
faith, but individual and conscious and private faith, was the
centre of the Anabaptist culture. The profound significance of
infant baptism as a function of the spiritual unity of the Church,
upon which Luther laid much stress, did not occur to them.
But it is quite clear that the excesses of Anabaptism were widely
attributed to Luther and the Protestants generally by those

B

who denounced them—and for that matter they still are so attributed, and falsely attributed. The historic role of Anabaptism was to provide a theme against which the Reformers could write counterpoint, a thesis to which they could provide an antithesis; it could almost be said that until the Anabaptists were ready, the Reformation could not be launched, for attempts at constitutional reformation had certainly been abortively made during the previous two or three centuries. The fact that Anabaptism has always been eccentric and relegated to the fringe of orthodox Church history is not a denial but a confirmation of their strange and vital part in the inception of the Confessional Reformation.

As we read the Confessions, then, we shall see in them the constitutive documents of Christian communions which regarded themselves as Churches, and which (with only one or two exceptions) genuinely hoped for at least a national Church which followed the Confessional teaching without dissent. The Confessions unite in denouncing Rome and Anabaptism. They unite in prescribing a theology and a Church order which they believe to be viable. Even as controversy in the fourth century produced a proliferation of creeds, each longer than its predecessor, which in the end were required to give way to an ecumenical creed, so the violent disputes of the sixteenth century produced a variety of Confessions, some of them very long indeed, which history has compelled to give way to the new approaches of the ecumenical movement. The difference is that whereas the fourth century had a Theodosius to 'establish' the 'Nicene Creed', the twentieth century has a paganism comparable with that of Augustus (and in places with that of Nero) which challenges the Church's preoccupations, and urges it to a new interpretation of the sacred phrase, 'Body of Christ', so that a world wider than Luther and Calvin dreamed of, and more indisputably in the power of the enemy than even they dared to judge, may yet be redeemed in the name of Christ.

But let it be understood that the age of the Confessions was an age of high tension—tension of a sort which without imagination a man of our own age can never comprehend. There is one doctrine which all the Confessions hold in common, and its rediscovery was the beginning of the Confessional age. This is the doctrine of Justification by Faith. It is a strictly Biblical doctrine, but what is new in the Confessional age is that it is elevated then for the first time to virtually credal status. Just what this doctrine is can be found by reading the first eight chapters of the Epistle to the Romans and then by following it through the Confessions which we are about to expound. But once Martin Luther had stated it uncompromisingly, nobody could ignore it. The question at bottom was: Is this, or is this not, a doctrine of credal status? Can a doctrine concerning the spiritual relation between men and God be regarded as essential to faith in the same sense in which the doctrines of the creeds had for fifteen hundred years been so regarded?

Like all those doctrines which are enshrined in the articles of the classic creeds, it must, once stated in this form, be subjected to rigorous scrutiny; the interpretation of one scholar must be challenged by another; that which is public and ubiquitous must be distinguished from that which is personal and local. All this went on in the ages when the creeds were fashioned: the Confessional age shows the same process at work in this doctrine. The Council of Trent was obliged, in its criticism, to state clearly what its position was in regard to it, and to direct the minds of the Catholic faithful towards what it held, after deliberation, to be right belief in respect of it. The Reformation came into being, however, for no other single reason than that Justification by Faith had become a living idea in the minds of Christians all over Europe. It is hardly too much to say that for all the Reformers, from the Anabaptists to Luther in his most conservative moments, Justification by Faith was a thirteenth credal article, even as its original expositor was the thirteenth apostle. No conviction at a less profound level than this, no insight less authentic into the essential truth of the Gospel, could have produced an age in which men were seriously prepared to found *Churches* on a dissent from Catholic principle. It is the essence of the Churches which produced the

Confessions that they thought of themselves as Churches, and could not regard themselves as sects: for they dissented (essentially, no matter at what peripheral points they also dissented) from the Catholic Church not in repudiating any credal belief that already stood, but in insisting on the incompleteness of the standing credal belief without this thirteenth article. And however much the Catholics were prepared to say by way of accommodation, the best they could say was that it was implied in the creeds and traditions of the Church. Disagreeing with this, and holding that it was not implied, or that it ought to be fully explicit, the Reformers broke away.

That is the dynamic principle of the Reformation. What followed was like an operation of drastic surgery. What we shall be dealing with in our final chapter may equally be likened to post-operational therapy. It is neither the business of this book, nor that of any commentator, to judge whether the Reformers were 'right', but what help we can gather as to the right course of action *now*, we must diligently look for.

II.—THE CONFESSION OF AUGSBURG, 1530

AFTER the nailing up of Luther's *Ninety-Five Theses* twelve years passed before the Emperor Charles V decided that he must return to Germany (after nine years' absence) to act as mediator in the religious controversies that Luther's gesture had generated. On 24 February 1530, Charles had received from the Pope the Imperial Crown, and his sympathies were wholly Catholic. None the less, he resolved to judge the matter impartially, hearing 'every man's opinion'. He accordingly summoned the Diet of Augsburg to meet on 8 April. At once the Elector of Saxony, on the advice of his Chancellor, Bruck, asked for a statement from the Protestant theologians.

Philip Melanchthon had already written an Apology to answer the charges of Johann Eck, an early friend but later enemy of Luther, made at Court. This Apology contained a statement of doctrine based on the Articles of Schwabach (October 1529). The document was sent to Luther, who replied, 'It pleases me well, and I know not how to better it . . . for I cannot tread so softly and gently.' On 25 June 1530 this document was presented over the signatures of two cities and seven princes, and was from that day known as the Confession of Augsburg. Its reception by the opposing party was by no means uniformly hostile; Melanchthon expressed himself willing to make certain amendments at their request; the Emperor was impatient of protracted negotiations and demanded submission, but none the less discussions continued for two months, in the course of which Eck made certain significant concessions from his side. But Luther was less patient than Charles, and repudiated Eck's concession, and in the end conformity was enjoined by Charles until a General Council should meet.

The Confession, together with certain modifications in the

Formula of Concord (see below, pp. 55-72) expresses the teaching to which the Lutheran Communion still officially conforms. It is therefore a document of high contemporary relevance. At certain points it is milder than what Luther would have written, and it should be compared with Luther's teaching on parallel points in his *Babylonish Captivity* and *Address to the German Nobility* of 1520. On the other hand, the difference in theological emphasis between it and the Calvinist Confessions will be evident when those are studied in Chapters V-VI below.

(See B. J. Kidd, *Documents of the Continental Reformation*, Nos. 112-113 (pp. 255-300), for a transcript of the Confession, and selections from related documents mentioned above.)

The First Part of the Augsburg Confession (1530), *entitled 'Articuli Fidei Praecipui'*

I. *Of God.* Concerning God the Father, the Confession affirms the Faith of the Holy Trinity, and describes the Eternal Father as 'Eternal, incorporeal, indivisible, of infinite power, wisdom and goodness, the creator and preserver of all things visible and invisible'. All unorthodox beliefs which contradict this are condemned: the Manicheans, who hold that a principle of evil is coeval with the principle of good, the Valentinians, Arians, Eunomians, Mahometans 'and all such' (*sc.* who believe doctrines that divide the Trinity), and the followers of Paul of Samosata 'both his original followers and their more recent imitators' who hold that the Word and the Spirit are not distinct persons, but that the Word is a 'word of mouth' and the Spirit a 'movement in the created world'. (This was the heresy classically described as Dynamic Monarchianism.)

II. *Of Original Sin.* 'After the fall of Adam all men begotten by the natural process of procreation are born in sin (*cum peccato*). That is, they are born without the fear of God, without a relation of confidence towards God (*fiducia erga Deum*), and with unholy desire (*concupiscentia*). This disease or fault in human origin is indeed sin, bringing with it condemnation and eternal death to those who are not reborn through baptism and the Holy Spirit.' The Pelagian heresy is condemned, with its doctrine that 'by his own strength' man can be 'justified' in the presence of God. By context, 'justification' means the restoration of the relation of 'fear and confidence' (*metus, fiducia*) and the uprooting of the 'unholy desire' (*concupiscentia*).

III. *Of the Son of God*. This article substantially reaffirms the 'Apostles' Creed', but has this significant addition after 'crucified, dead and buried': '... that he might reconcile the Father to us, and be an offering not only for the sin of our origin but also for all actual human sins' (*pro omnibus hominum peccatis*). And after 'sitteth at the right hand of God the Father': '... that he may reign for ever and have dominion over all creatures, and sanctify those who believe in him by the sending of the Holy Spirit into their hearts to guide and console them and to give them life and to defend them against the devil and the power of sin'.

IV. *Of Justification*. 'Men cannot be justified in the presence of God by their own strength, deserts or works, but are justified freely (*gratis*) through Christ by faith (*propter Christum per fidem*), when they wholly believe that they are received into grace and that through Christ their sins are forgiven, for as much as by his death Christ has made satisfaction for our sins. This faith God imputes for righteousness in his own sight.' It must be noted that whenever the word *credo* is used in such a context as this, it means much more than what is meant in modern conversational use by the word 'believe'. Nowadays 'I believe' means 'I am not certain', or 'I put this tentatively'. In the language of Luther (and in the corresponding language of St. Paul) it always means, 'I commit myself to this'. More amply paraphrased it means, 'I withhold my claim for proof and my right to be persuaded by evidences, and I act on the assumption that this is true'. Hence we must translate at least by 'wholly believe'.

V. *Of the Church's Ministry*. The ministry of teaching the Gospel and providing the sacraments is instituted that we may hold and follow these doctrines. The Word and Sacraments are the 'instruments' by which the Holy Spirit is given; but the gift is given not because of the *act* of preaching of administering the sacraments but because of the *justification* effected by Christ. The Anabaptists' opinion that the Spirit can be received without outward speech or action is condemned.

VI. *Of the New Obedience.* The purpose of this short article is to make clear that it is not by the giving or receiving of the Sacraments *per se* that justification and forgiveness are achieved. Faith should 'bring forth good fruits' and the doing of the commandments of God is the consequence of God's, not our own, goodwill.

VII. *Of the Church.* 'One holy Church will remain for ever. The Church is the congregation of saints in which the Gospel is rightly taught and the Sacraments are rightly administered. For the true unity of the Church it is sufficient that there be agreement concerning the teaching of the Gospel and the administration of the Sacraments, but it is not necessary that the same human traditions be everywhere observed, in as much as they are rites or ceremonies instituted by men.'

VIII. *Of the Nature of the Church.* In this article it is provided that the imperfection of its ministers does not invalidate the sacraments they dispense, and the Donatist and other heresies, which take the opposite view, are condemned.

IX. *Of Baptism.* Baptism is 'necessary to salvation' and through it the grace of God is offered. Children should be baptized in order that, 'offered to God, they may be received into God's grace'. The Anabaptist opinion that it is improper to baptize infants, and that infants unbaptized can inherit salvation, is condemned. (It is not here openly said that children who die unbaptized are lost to grace: but it is clearly implied.)

X. *Of the Lord's Supper.* 'The body and blood of Christ are truly present (*vere adsint*), and are distributed in the Lord's Supper to those who partake; we repudiate all who teach otherwise.'

XI. *Of Confession.* The retention of private absolution in the Confessional is recommended, provided that it is understood that 'it is not necessary that all sins whatever be enumerated in Confession; for this is impossible, as the Psalmist says, "Who can tell his offences?" '.

XII. *Of Penitence*. Those who have fallen into sin after baptism may at any time be converted and be regarded as truly penitent. To all such, the church should dispense absolution. In Penitence there are, however, two distinct parts: *contrition* —sorrow for sin—and *faith*—acceptance of Christ's gift of forgiveness. The good works which follow are the 'fruits of repentance'. The Anabaptists are in error where they teach that a man once justified can never lose the Holy Spirit, and when they teach that any man can in this life attain such perfection as to be unable to commit sin; and the Novatianists are in error when they decline to receive back into the Church people who after baptism and confession of faith have fallen into sin but have shown that they repent. But worse than all are those who claim that by any work of our own we can make satisfaction for sin or claim forgiveness. These things are of Christ alone.

XIII. *Of the Use of the Sacraments*. 'The sacraments are instituted, not only that they may be signs of the Christian profession among men, but much more that they may be signs and testimonies of the goodwill of God towards us, offered to us for the stirring up and confirming of the faith of those who make use of them. Therefore the sacraments should be so used that faith may have free course (*accedat*), faith which believes in the promises that the sacraments hold forth and display. Therefore we condemn all those who teach that the sacraments offer justification in their own right (*ex opere operato*—literally, 'in consequence of the thing done'), and who neglect to teach that faith is required in the use of the Sacraments, faith that believes that sins are forgiven.' The error here condemned is, of course, the Roman doctrine that in the receiving of the sacrament itself there is merit without any consideration of faith. Without faith, says the Confession, the operation is entirely empty.

XIV. *Of The Church's Orders*. 'Nobody may preach publicly

in the church or administer the sacraments except he be duly
called (*rite vocatus*).'

XV. *Of the Church's Rites.* 'Let those rites be kept which can
be observed without sin, and which promote the Church's
peace and good order: such are certain holy days, festivals and
so forth.' But no conscience must be burdened on this matter,
and no observance (*sc.* apart from the two Sacraments and
the normal daily offices) must be regarded as necessary to
salvation. Any human custom which claims to placate God or
to offer satisfaction or grace of itself is contrary to the Gospel
and the faith. Vows, fasting and the observance of days have
no effect towards salvation, and if they are so represented they
defy the teaching of the Gospel.

XVI. *Of Civil Affairs.* This article is designed to refute those
who believe that Christians must take no part in civil life and
contract no social obligations. It is lawful, says the Confession,
for a Christian to be a magistrate or a judge in the service of
the State; he may 'appoint punishments for wrongdoers, he
may declare war and serve as a soldier, enter into a legal
contract, hold property, swear an oath at the bidding of the
magistrate, and marry'. The Anabaptists, believing that
Christians must not engage in these social relations, are once
again condemned. So are all those who imagine that refusal to
bear public office advances a man in the sight of God. Only the
fear of God and faith (*timor et fides*) does that. The Christian
Way does not 'undermine the fabric of the state and its
economy; on the contrary it demands that it be preserved as
an ordinance of God, and that in all such relations, charity be
exercised'. Hence, it is right that Christians should be law-
abiding citizens and respect the ordinances of secular authority.

XVII. *Of Christ's Return in Judgment.* As the Creed says,
Christians believe that Christ will return in judgment. It is
here added that the elect will be appointed to eternal bliss, and
the impenitent and the blasphemers to eternal torment. The
Latin for the last two substantives is *impios ac diabolos.*
Diaboli carries its ancient meaning of 'slanderers' or (in the
context) 'blasphemers'. The whole expression means those

who have deliberately and impenitently refused grace, not, of course, those who have ignorantly or carelessly done wrong. The Anabaptist view is again impugned; their position is that the infidels and blasphemers are punished, but for a limited time; the Confession insists that the punishment is eternal. Another error is ascribed to those who say that after the resurrection of the dead the godly will rule this world, and the ungodly will be punished in this world. Against this view (described as *Iudaica opinio*) the Confession holds that the punishment is strictly of the eternal world, and not of the temporal.

XVIII. *Of Free Will.* 'Human will has a certain freedom for the effecting of human justice and the discernment of those things which are subject to reason. But without the Holy Spirit it has no power to effect God's justice or spiritual justice, because "mortal man perceives not the things that are of God's Spirit".' It is therefore an error to say (as do the Pelagians) that a man can with the unaided use of his natural faculties choose God above all things. Nature can achieve 'external acts' (such as keeping a man from theft or murder), but it cannot achieve 'inward motions' (such as the fear of God, a relation of confidence towards God, chastity, patience).

XIX. *Of the Cause of Sin.* 'Although God creates and preserves nature, the cause of sin is the will of the evil ones— of the devil and of the ungodly—a will which turns away from God of itself, not which is turned away by God.' (Only so can we render the force of *quae, non adiuvante Deo, avertit se a Deo.*)

XX. *Of Faith and Good Works.* This is the first article which does not begin with a sentence whose main verb is *docent* (if we except V and VIII, both of which are virtually continuations of the preceding articles). It begins with a controversial point. 'Our people are falsely charged with prohibiting good works.' Of its long argument most may here be briefly summarized, but one important section will be quoted in full.

(§§ 1-2) 'The accusation that we interdict good works is unfounded. It is true that whereas the preaching of the Church has degenerated into the giving of homilies concerning childish and peripheral matters (*puerilia et non necessaria*), such as pilgrimages, the cult of saints, rosaries, fast-days, etc., our preaching deals with faith. Indeed, in mentioning faith, we break a long and scandalous silence which the Church has up to now maintained.'

(§§ 3-6) 'The matter on which the Church has kept this deep silence (*altissimum silentium*) is that no *works* of our own can reconcile God to us. To believe that they can is to devalue (*aspernere*) the work and grace of Christ. This is no new doctrine. It is unambiguously stated by Paul, and the Fathers are full of it' (Augustine is mentioned and Ambrose is quoted).

Now follows § 7: 'Although this doctrine (*sc.* of faith) is scorned by those who have no religious experience (*ab imperitis*), men of pious and abased (*pavidae*) conscience know in their own experience that it brings abundant consolation; no conscience can be given peace by any works, only by faith. Peace comes from the sure knowledge that through Christ they stand reconciled with God (*habent placatum Deum*). . . . The whole of this doctrine must be referred to the situation of the conscience in a crisis of terror (*ad illud certamen perterrefactae conscientiae*), and it cannot be understood except in that context. It is idle for men who have no religious experience, profane persons, to judge of it; to such men Christian justice can merely appear in civil and philosophical terms.'

In § 9 the argument is continued. In former days the doctrine of works drove men to wild asceticisms that they might satisfy its demands. Different people devised different methods of satisfying God's demands by works. There was, then (§ 10), a great need that the doctrine of faith be revived. Be it observed, however, that by faith we mean (§ 11) not merely assent to a story (*historiae notitiam*), but belief in the story, and belief in the effect of the story—namely, in the actual forgiveness of our sins by Christ. The man (§ 12) who understands that he is reconciled to God (*habet propitium Patrem*) through Christ, truly knows God, and knows that he is in God's care. Those who do not hold the doctrine of faith have no understanding of the forgiveness of sins: 'they hate God as though he were their enemy, they do not call on him, they expect no good from him'. This we say (§ 13) on the authority of Augustine and of Scripture.

Given this (§§ 14-16), we can say that good works are the Christian's duty. But except they be under the direction of the Holy Spirit, they will not be good works at all, because we are, apart from the grace of Christ, in the hands of the devil. The devil inspires in men both evil acts and wrong intellectual attitudes (*opiniones*). In sum, our teaching should not be charged with making good works impossible. It is the only teaching that makes them possible—as Christ said, 'Without me, ye can do nothing', and as the Church's hymn (*sc.* of the Holy Spirit) says,

> Where thou art not, man hath nought;
> Every holy deed and thought
> Comes from thy Divinity[1]

XXI. *Of the Cult of the Saints.* 'It is right that the memory of the saints be kept before us, that we may imitate their faith and good works in our own calling, as the Emperor may imitate David in waging war to drive out the Turks from our country. Both the Emperor and David are kings. But Scripture does not teach us that we should invoke the saints or ask for their help: Christ alone is set forth there as our mediator, reconciler, priest and intercessor. He must be invoked, and he has promised to hear our prayers; that worship he entirely approves which invokes his aid in all troubles.'

XXII. *Summary.* Our doctrine is scriptural, and is in accordance with the teaching of all the classic authors of the Catholic Church. We are no heretics. We contend only that abuses prevail, and that these have crept into the Church without any clear authority. In any case the authority for insisting on uniformity of usage in the Church is so dubious

---

[1] Extracted from J. M. Neale's translation of *Veni sancte Spiritus* (see *English Hymnal*, 155), three lines of which are quoted in Latin in the Confession at this point.

that it were better for the Bishops to accept our Confession. The ancient customs of the Church are not set aside in our liturgical use, except for certain abuses about which there has been public complaint; these have been corrected according to the promptings of a good conscience—but that is all.

The Second Part, entitled 'Articuli in quibus recensentur abusus mutati'

Here are seven long articles, expanding the final sentence of Part I. These are devoted to Communion in Both Kinds, the Marriage of Priests, the Mass, Confession, the Distinctions of Fasts and other Traditions, Monastic Vows, and the Power of the Church. They may be summarized as follows.

The ground of these changes is stated in the preamble as the *conscience of the people*; this picks up the expression *publica querela*, 'the people's complaint', in the closing article of Part I. The Catholics are charged with contempt of the rights of the ordinary Christian in perpetuating the practices which the Lutherans call 'abuses'.

I. *Of Communion in Both Kinds*, it is simply pointed out that Scripture (Matt. xxvi. 27) expressly enjoins the distribution of the cup to the people, and that therefore the Church's withholding of it is contrary to the will of Christ. It cannot be properly argued that Christ's words to the apostles in that passage are to be applied now to the priesthood only, because Paul in 1 Cor. xi. 24 clearly teaches otherwise. Among the Fathers, Cyprian and Jerome, and among the earlier Popes Gelasius, expressly bid the people to take the cup. The Roman practice is neither ancient, nor scriptural, nor convenient.

II. *Of the Marriage of Priests* it is argued first that Scripture permits clerical marriage (2 Tim. iii. 2), and second that to prohibit it is contrary to that created nature which is of God's design, and which it is impudence in man to presume to alter. Two historical precedents are mentioned—how Pius I was reported as saying that while there were arguments in favour of clerical celibacy, those in favour of clerical marriage were much stronger; and how, when four hundred years before an archbishop of Mainz had attempted to enforce celibacy in Germany not merely by prohibiting clerical marriage for the future but also by annulling marriages already contracted by priests, he caused a civil riot from which he barely escaped with his life (§ 5).[1]

Celibacy, however desirable it may be in some eyes, is an institution to which human nature will not stand up (§ 6). 'As the world grows older, human nature seems to grow weaker' (*ibid.*), and the Church may expect the supply of priests to dry up if celibacy is enforced.

And further (§ 7), the legal enforcement of celibacy induces scandal because of those who being legally celibate satisfy their desires in ways that are natural but impious. Nothing else can be expected when so unnatural a law is enforced. It is wrong to enact a law whose enforcement cannot be either practically certain or naturally justified. It is (§ 8) highly scandalous that men be punished, even with death, for nothing but entering into the honourable estate of marriage.

III. *Of the Mass* it is first protested that the Lutheran Churches do not abolish the Mass. 'The Mass is retained among us, and celebrated with the utmost reverence.' Almost all the ancient rites are preserved—but we add some German hymns to the traditional Latin ones, for the edifying of the simple, and the vernacular tongue is used for the same reason (§ 1). The people are more fully instructed (§ 2) before they are admitted to the Sacrament than used to be the case—but this is proper, and tends to an increase of the benefits they gain from it (§ 3).

It is contended (§§ 4-5) without reserve that abuses have prevailed in the celebration of the Mass, and that these chiefly gather about the association of the Sacrament with money. Therefore the practice of private masses has been abandoned; the association of these with monetary payment has proved a corruption worthy to be condemned under Paul's stern injunction in 1 Cor. xi. 26. No sacred matter has been brought into such disrepute as the Mass, and had the bishops corrected

[1] The paragraphing is not original: it is here given as in Kidd's *Documents of the Continental Reformation.*

what they knew to be prevalent abuses, the present controversy might never have arisen (§§ 6-7).

The Roman custom (§§ 8-10) has been to multiply masses, on the theory that while the satisfaction wrought by Christ in his Passion was for original sin, the Mass is an act (*opus*) which provides satisfaction for daily sins. But it is held on the Protestant side that the offering of Christ was not only for original sin but for all sins whatever. The Epistle to the Hebrews confirms this doctrine. (Heb. x. 11-13, in which the word 'Once' is emphasized; it is upon this word that the Protestant argument here hinges.)

Since Scripture clearly teaches that we are justified by faith (§ 10), the Mass must not be so presented as to appear in itself a justification for sin, or for sins, *ex opere operato* (simply by the act of celebrating and receiving it). Without faith it is meaningless.

But (§12) since Christ commanded that the Sacrament be celebrated 'in memory of him', the Protestant interprets the Sacrament as a means by which faith is nourished in the heart, and the terrified conscience is consoled and lifted up (*erigat et consoletur pavida conscientia*). 'For this is remembering Christ: to call to mind, *and to feel* his benefits.' It is not sufficient to remember the story. There must be *faith* (§ 13).

Since the Mass is of this kind (as Protestants see it), it is sufficient (§ 14) that one public Mass be celebrated each Sunday, and on other days as may be required. Private masses are not needed. There is no ancient authority for the multiplication of celebrations: Paul, Chrysostom and the Nicene canons all witness the other way. Therefore (§§ 16-17) the charge that the Protestants are abusing the Mass cannot lie against them. It is only that at certain points the rite is altered to avoid abuse, and that the number of masses said is greatly reduced.

IV. *Of Confession* it is similarly shown that the Protestants have not abolished it, but only altered its mode and practice. Absolution is indeed necessary before the Sacrament can be rightly taken, and (§ 1) absolution must be, and is among Protestants, pronounced in the name of God. The Power of

the Keys belongs to the Church and must be exercised (§ 2).
But (§ 3) the Protestants do not believe that the medieval
emphasis on *satisfactions* is for edification. That has resulted in
a mode of confession which makes no mention of faith in the
satisfaction of Christ. As was said above, in Part I, XI (§§ 4-6),
the enumeration of personal sins is not only not necessary, but
conducive to a false moral sense: nobody can know the extent
of his sins. But he can know the infinite extent of Christ's
power to forgive.

V. *On Fast Days* and kindred subjects the argument runs
thus: the popular opinion (which is shared also by many of the
learned) is that the human act of distinguishing foods (*dis-
crimina ciborum*)—certain foods to be eaten on certain days:
fish on Friday, for example—is a human act which will procure
grace and forgiveness of our sins. From this (§§ 1-2) many
disorders have arisen. (1) The primacy of faith is once more
obscured; (2) our apprehension of God's natural order is
distorted; (3) a multiplicity of observances has perplexed
those who attempted the impossible task of keeping them
all.

(Argument (2) above needs explanation. If the observance
of fasts, and distinctions of foods, was held in honour, the
natural vocations of human beings tended to be dishonoured.
It was more important in such circles that fish and not meat
be eaten on Friday than that a man should educate his
children, a wife should be a good wife, a governor should be a
good governor (*paterfamilias educabat sobolem, mater pariebat,
princeps regebat rempublicam*). People who were married, or
held public offices, were troubled in their consciences because
the life 'in the world' was thus dishonoured, and looked with
uncomfortable envy on the life of the cloister. One prong of the
argument seems directed at the Catholics, the other at the
Anabaptists.)

It has turned out (§§ 10-11) that the time spent on the
examination and invention of these trifles has been taken from
the time that should have been spent by councils and clergy
on the investigation of the ultimate doctrines of the Church

C

(utiliorem doctrinam, de fide, de cruce, de spe, de dignitate civilium rerum, de consolatione conscientiarum in arduis tentationibus).

If, as Protestants hold, (§ 12) the doctrine of justification by faith is primary, it was necessary to disabuse the minds of the simple of doctrines so apt to confuse them. If Protestants teach that no merit attaches to the keeping of such observances, Scripture is on their side (§§ 13-17). And if Protestants are charged with devaluing discipline and the mortification of the flesh (§ 18), they answer that they preach Christ crucified, and faith in his cross, which implies 'being crucified with him'. This they hold to be a sufficient answer. As concerns personal discipline (§ 19), they teach that every Christian should so moderate his life as to be free from those temptations to sin which come either from satiety or from the need induced by undue rigour. Therefore (§ 20) fasting in itself is not discouraged; but fasting by tradition, on given days, and as a means of procuring merit in the sight of God, is to Protestants abhorrent. Protestants keep many traditions, but with them liberty of conscience and local use, that their appropriate use may be more effective than their legal and indiscriminate imposition (§§ 22-4).

VI. *Of Monastic Vows*, the argument begins with a reference to the difference between the 'free associations' (*libera collegia*) which were monasteries in the time of Augustine (§ 1) and the corrupt institutions which in later times they became (§ 2). What began as a freely accepted discipline has now become a rigorous and arbitrary servitude (§§ 3-5). So much for that which takes place within monasteries. But in addition there is now a tradition that taking vows is comparable with baptism, and is the best way to secure merit (§ 6), and indeed some say that vows are a more effective way of gaining merit than baptism (§ 7), so that what began as institutions for the pursuit of learning and prayer (§§ 8-9) have become places in which it is assumed that alone the good life can be lived. This in turn leads to a disparagement of marriage (§§ 10-12).

Again (§ 13), a man under vows is bound by them as if by

the law of God; but in practice it has been found necessary to provide the Supreme Pontiff with the right of dispensation. Then are vows, or are they not, to be regarded as simply equal in authority with God's own commandment? (§§ 14-15).

Furthermore (§§ 16-17), it must be clear that vows are often taken without due forethought or warning by young men and women who cannot know what they are undertaking. Any kind of persuasion to take vows, including the hidden moral persuasion implied in the extolling of the monastic life, is deceitful and contrary to the will of God. Canon Law in several places forbids the taking of vows before the age of fifteen (§ 18), and in one place the age is raised to eighteen. But too many have been received who, according to these canons, should not have been (see below, p. 52).

Finally (§§ 19-33), the whole principle of vows is liable to the charge of vanity, in as much as the votive system may degenerate into a man-made device for securing merit (§ 20). The unnatural climate of the monastic system tends to produce from its devotees such doctrine as that man-made devices can procure salvation (*facticiae religiones satisfaciant pro peccatis*) (§§ 22-7). The notion that only monks are in a state of perfection (§§ 28-30) has wrought untold scandal among the ordinary people of the Church. Celibacy, poverty and sackcloth have nothing to do with the state of perfection (§ 29). Flight from the world into a monastery has nothing to do with perfection (§ 31). The people must be told this, and (§§ 32-3) the vanity of the false tradition of monasticism exposed.

VII. *Of the Power of the Church*, and especially of bishops, it is argued first that much confusion has arisen because three kinds of power have been confused in controversy power of the Church, power of bishops, and 'the power of the sword'. Wars and discord have arisen because Popes have attempted to wrest from secular princes power to which the Church was never entitled. It must then be understood clearly (§§ 1-6) that the power committed by Christ to his Church, whether to the whole body or to individuals, is a power that is not of this world. The Power of the Keys operates in the world of 'eternal justice, the Holy Spirit, eternal life' (§ 4). When Church power occupies itself with eternal things, it does not interfere with secular power, whose business is with worldly things. The secular prince is in charge, not of men's minds, but of their bodies and property, and bodily sanctions are within his field that the civil peace may be kept.

But (§§ 7-8) the two spheres must never be confused. Church power begins and ends with the preaching of the Gospel and the administering of the Sacraments. It must never break into the field of the secular power, deal in earthly dominion, repeal laws made by princes, withdraw legitimate civil obedience, stand in the way of judicial processes, or make laws concerning the administration of the secular state. If the bishop holds any power of the sword, he has it not from the Gospel (§ 9) but from a human hand. The proper power of a bishop includes the preaching of the Word and administering of the Sacraments, the scrutiny of Church teaching and the rejection of what is not in conformity with the Gospel, and the exclusion from the Church of those who live in open sin: but this exclusion must be by word, not by force (§§ 10-11). But if they themselves teach what is contrary to the Gospel (§§ 12-13), no obedience is due to them. Any other jurisdiction that a bishop may have, such as in the matter of marriage, or of tithes, he has from a human, not a divine source.

The power of the bishops to institute ceremonies (§§ 15-40) is a matter of great controversy. Those who attribute to them such power support their argument from incidents in Scripture where the Apostles are recorded as taking decisions in the name of the Church (as in Acts xv, and especially on the text John xvi. 12-13). But the Protestant contention is that no bishop has authority to institute anything that is manifestly contrary to the Gospel (§ 17). Many traditions are in fact contrary to it (§ 18), as for example that which ascribes virtues to certain foods, certain observances of days, and so forth. Indeed (§ 19), any legal imposition of this kind is unscriptural, and therefore outside the competence of the bishop to direct. Church institutions of any kind (§ 26) are tolerable only in as much as they are, and are seen to be, instituted simply for the good order of the Church.

Observances, then (§ 27), may be kept by the Church provided that their keeping or neglect is not made a matter of sin and salvation. But (for example) it is an error to believe that the Lord's Day, Easter and Pentecost are enjoined on the Church *as observances* by divine authority, even though they are based on the teaching of Scripture itself (§ 28). Scripture expressly removes 'the sabbath' from the realm of law (§ 29). There is no ceremony or observance of any kind (§ 30) which can be said to have been enjoined on the Church by Christ. Any such argument is always an indication that the essential justice and liberty of the Christian has been forgotten (§§ 31-2). If it be argued (§ 33) that the Apostles directed the Church to 'abstain from blood' (Acts xv. 20) it must be answered that they were especially careful to avoid the appearance of imposing what would be a burden to any man's conscience (see verse 19). And in fact that commandment is not now regarded as binding on Christians. It could be shown (§ 34) that very few Church canons are in fact observed to the letter. Therefore (§ 35) obedience can rightly be claimed by bishops only in so far as their commands do not involve the extinction of a good conscience. The imposition of celibacy is an example of a command that offends in this way. The Churches are not asking the bishops to 'patch up an appearance of concord by the sacrifice of their honour' (*honoris sui iactura sarciant concordiam*), but only that they refrain from imposing intolerable burdens on the conscience (§ 36). Institutions of one age may not be suitable to another (§ 37), and some seem to have come into being through error (§ 38). It would be well if the Pope of his goodness would relax these burdens (§§ 38-40), but if that cannot be, then 'we must obey God rather than men'. Protestants do not wish to withdraw all obedience from bishops, but they want the pure Gospel set forth, and the inhibitions to its free course removed.

Epilogue to the Confession. 'In laying stress on these principal articles of our controversy, we say nothing of other abuses which we deplore—of indulgences, pilgrimages and improper excommunications; of visitations, and of the strife between monks and secular clergy concerning parish rights, confessions, burials, extra-ordinary meetings, and innumerable other things. These we pass over, that the great concern for which we contend may more clearly be apprehended, a concern which is expressed not for the vilifying of any person, but for the good order of the Church.'

Comment on the Augsburg Confession will be confined here to a consideration of three key-words which are prominent in it.

1. *Faith* (*fides*). The whole of the first phase of the Reformation Controversy turned on the word 'faith'. The controversy was (it need hardly be said) a great deal more than a linguistic dispute; but this is how it took its first linguistic form. The origin of the controversy can be found in a Scriptural ambiguity. Romans v. 1 opens with the words, 'Now that we have been justified through faith, let us continue at peace with God'. 1 Cor. xiii ends with the words, 'In a word, there are three things that last for ever: faith, hope and love; but the greatest of them all is love' (verse 13).

If your question is 'What is the word in which can be summed up that quality in the whole man which alone is indispensable to justification?', Luther's answer is 'faith', using the word as Paul uses it in the first passage. If your question is 'What is the first of the three co-eternal theological virtues?', the answer is 'faith' in the second sense. When the Council of Trent denied the Lutheran teaching, it denied it on the ground of the second meaning of faith (see below, p. 42); in effect, it said 'faith is a powerful belief, but not a certainty: therefore in thinking you are justified you may be wrong'. In its anxiety to refute what it believed to be a dangerous subjectivity in the Lutheran teaching, the Council did not merely attack it as though it were using 'faith' in the sense of 1 Cor. xiii. 13, but overshot the mark in attacking it as though it were using it in the sense of 'human faith', which by St. Thomas Aquinas (S.T. Ia IIae LXII 4) is clearly distinguished from the theological virtue of faith.

The distinction which ought to have been made there was clearly made in *The King's Book* (1543), for which see below, pp. 99-102.

In Luther's teaching, however, 'faith', in the Romans v. 1 sense, is a quality of the whole man, not a quality that is to his credit, but a quality given to him by God through the action of the Holy Spirit. In this sense there is nothing subjective about it; yet in the sense that it is *his own*, that it provides a means by which he can personally (with his whole person) respond to the Act of God in Justification, it is subjective, and rightly so. At another point, that of 'works', Trent accused the Reformers of too little attention to subjective merit, and to the power for good of the human will. But here again Trent missed the true contention of the Reformers. For they were not saying that faith is a subjective belief, and neither were they saying that works can never be good or creditable. What they did insist on was that faith is God-given, and becomes what in modern speech we would call a 'new dimension' of life; that outside that 'new dimension' the quality of our 'works' can make no difference to our standing with God, because we have no standing with him *ex hypothesi*; and that once the 'new dimension' is the habitual mode of our life, 'good works' brought about by 'free will' are not thought of by their agent as creditable, because the will of God is what he wants to do. He may fall away—he certainly will, humanly speaking—but in so far as he is 'in the sphere of God's grace, where we now stand' (Rom. v. 2) the whole system of gaining credit for doing duties becomes irrelevant and even ludicrous. Once love is there (and he is doing what he loves doing), the idea of getting credit for it is laughable: indeed it was his doctrine of grace and justification which generated in Luther that 'laughter' which to his enemies (and to not a few even of his friends) seemed to be theological irresponsibility.

2. *Justice* (*iustitia*). Justice is primarily an attribute of God. It is misleading to think of it at all in terms of human justice, which means normally a fair return for a service, or a deserved punishment for a misdemeanour. With that it has nothing to

do. Justice in the theological sense is absolute, and means 'straightness', or, almost, 'perfection'. Justice as a relation between persons (e.g. between God and ourselves) is a relation of perfect confidence, of uninhibited conversation, of habitual intimacy which transcends any notion of 'fair play', but which at the same time presupposes that the two are on equal terms.

But God and man could not conceivably be on less equal terms. God is perfect and we are not merely wrongdoers; we have in us an inborn fear and hatred of perfection. If it is God's purpose to hold intimate, confidential conversation with us, He may not *pretend* that we are good when we are evil; but He can, and does, and in Christ showed that He does, treat us as though we were fit to be trusted. This is the imputation of justice (or righteousness) to us. The purpose of this imputation is that we shall be *made* fit for conversation with God, i.e. *justified*. By a miracle which nobody can explain, but all must adore, God imputes righteousness to man, and makes it possible for man to be freed from the bondage of fear and hatred of the good, and to enjoy the good, and thus to walk with God as with a friend. Justification by 'faith alone', then is a formula representing the end which is God's purpose, and the condition through which alone it may be met.

3. *Conscientia*. At several points this word appears in the Augsburg Confession. It especially appears in XX 7, and in § 12 of the section on the Mass in Part II. It appears here with qualifying adjectives such as *pavida, perterrefacta*; and it is used of the humble and pious conscience which is overridden by Romish abuses. The reader will find it instructive in this connexion to read chapter 8 of Professor C. S. Lewis's *Studies in Words* (1960); although not all of the material given there is relevant here, he will be aware after reading it of the dangerous ambiguity that lies within this word. The ambiguity can first be found in the fact that the word from which 'conscience' is derived in Latin and Greek can mean both 'sharing a secret with another' or 'holding secret knowledge within oneself'. It is a special development of the second meaning that is now always attached to conscience in ordinary speech; and

in the religious writing of the sixteenth and seventeenth centuries the word, whether in Latin or in English, could already connote a certain 'privacy of judgment' which was especially abhorrent to the teaching of the Roman Catholic Church.

It is however misleading to read that meaning primarily into *conscientia* as Luther used it and as the Augsburg Confession uses it. For them, *conscientia* is a knowledge concerning oneself which a man shares with no other man, but which he does share with God. The conscience in a man who is at the very point of justification (moving, as it were, from one dimension to the other) is *pavida* or *perterrefacta* because he is conscious of his own guilt and unworthiness for the first time, and conscious also of the prodigious nature of the gift that he is to receive. It is wrong to say that this means that he personally judges himself to be guilty and about to receive a blessing. Luther undoubtedly meant, and caused to be written into the Confession, that he has received this knowledge from God; that God and he share it; that this sharing is all part of the process of justification. It follows that the Eucharist is a comfort to the terrified conscience, that the doctrine of *sola fide* is the only help of a troubled conscience, and that the abuses which have corrupted the threefold relation between man, the Church and God under the late medieval papacy are an offence to the conscience in that man is debarred from the opportunity of sharing anything at all with God, even self-knowledge.

A misunderstanding concerning words naturally led some to appropriate too much to the human judgment, and others to ascribe this excess to teachers who did not intend it. The most considerable analyses of conscience (in the modern sense) and its relation to the work of Justification are to be found in the writings of the English Puritan divines, especially those of John Owen and Thomas Goodwin (see below, p. 124).

III.—THE COUNCIL OF TRENT,[1] 1545-63

THE Council of Trent, summoned for the reformation of the Papal Church (which is commonly called the 'Counter-Reformation') held twenty-five sessions during the years 1545-7, 1551-2 and 1562-3, during which every aspect of the Church's life and doctrine was examined. The Council promulgated decrees, canons and decrees of Reformation, which are published in its Minutes. The Decrees represent the mind of the Council on doctrine: the Canons translate this (where necessary) into regulations and anathemas to which posterity can refer; the Decrees of Reformation concern the administration of the Church's offices, finances, orders and dioceses.

That this was a radical reformation of doctrine and manners is at once evident. That it tacitly admits many of the charges made in the writings of Luther and in the Augsburg Confession to have weight is equally evident. But at most points it judged the charges misdirected, and in all the major points of doctrinal contention on the Reformers' part, it judged the Reformers mistaken and heretical.[2]

Much of the Council's business was domestic and controversial only within the Roman Catholic Church. We shall here attend to those points where its findings bear on points raised in the Augsburg Confession. It must be borne in mind that only the Augsburg Confession[3], of those which came to have any ecumenical significance and authority, had been published by

---

[1] See J. Waterworth (ed.), *The Canons and Decrees of the Council of Trent* (1848); B. J. Kidd, *The Counter-Reformation* (1936, chs. 3-4).

[2] What is now called the Roman Catholic Church is the Communion that is bound by the Council of Trent. It is, of course, an error to refer to the Medieval Church of the West as 'Roman Catholic', since, as Bernard Manning has said, 'The Medieval Church is the mother of us all.' The Roman Catholic Church is a reformed, or counter-reformed Church.

[3] The Augsburg Confession is here and hereafter referred to as *A* and the proceedings of the Council of Trent as *T*.

the time when the Council first met, and that Calvin's *Institutes* had appeared only in the first three (1536, 1539, 1541) of its five editions.[1]

At the first doctrinal session (Session III, 4 February 1546) the Council affirmed its belief in the 'Nicene Creed' as authoritative, and at Session IV (8.4.46)[2] it declared its mind on the Holy Scriptures. 'The purity of the Gospel', they said, 'must be preserved in the Church, which Gospel, promised before through the prophets in the Holy Scriptures, our Lord Jesus Christ, the Son of God, first promulgated with his own mouth, and then commanded to be preached by his Apostles to every living creature as the fountain both of saving truth and of moral discipline.' The Council enumerated the Books of the Old and New Testament, including in the Old Testament Tobit, Judith, Wisdom, Sirach, Baruch and the two books of Maccabees. Luther's teaching was that the Apocryphal Books were not canonical; but no enumeration is made in *A*.

A's doctrine of *Original Sin* (II) finds an answer in *T*, Session V (17.6.46). What is there written may be briefly summarized in these words: that Adam lost the holiness and rectitude in which he had been constituted, and incurred the wrath of God, death, and captivity to the devil; that he lost this holiness and rectitude not only for himself but for all his posterity; that not human power, but only the merit of Jesus Christ, can restore what Adam lost; that baptism is not only for the remission of sins but for the taking away of this original sin, and therefore infants should be baptized 'that they may be cleansed by regeneration of that which they contracted by generation'; but that in the baptized there remains 'concupiscence' or a tendency to sin, which is not properly to be called sin, though it is 'of sin' and 'inclines to sin'. The Virgin Mary alone of mortals is exempt from the taint of original sin.

Except for its last clause, this contains nothing offensive to

---

[1] The *Institutes* had been through all five editions (including those of 1550 and 1559) and thirteen printings in French and Latin before the Council was finally prorogued.

[2] Date of the Session: so throughout this chapter.

the followers of *A*, although the necessity of Baptism for salvation here implied, which *A* accepts, would not be agreeable to the mind of the Calvinistic Confessions (see below, p. 85).

The Tridentine doctrine of *Justification* is expounded in the proceedings of Session VI (13.1.47). In its account of this the Council produced a treatise in sixteen chapters followed by thirty-three brief Canons.

The condition to which man is reduced by the Fall, they write (§ 1), is such as to have enslaved all men, Jew and Gentile alike. Christ was sent (§ 2) to liberate both the Jews who were under the Law and the Gentiles who 'followed not after justice, Rom. ix. 30'. He died for all men, but not all receive the benefit of his death (§ 3); only those receive it who are born again in Christ, and they may be thankful (Col. i. 12-14). The washing of regeneration is required (§ 4) for this translation from a state of sin to a state of grace.

The process of justification begins with Election (§ 5): that is, the sinner is called by God's prevenient grace, without any merit on his part. Thereafter they can assent to and co-operate with this grace. His free will cannot move him to justification in the sight of God, but it can assent to the promptings of the Spirit, and can conversely reject them. Disposed by the Spirit towards this righteousness (§ 6), by turning themselves towards it they grow into a state in which they begin to hate sin and place their faith and hope in God. This moves them to baptism, or to conversion.

All this (§ 8) is preparation. Justification follows, being not only the remission of sins but also the sanctification and renewal of the inward man. The final cause of Justification is the glory of God and life everlasting; the efficient cause is our merciful God who washes, sanctifies, seals and anoints us with his Spirit; the meritorious cause is the atonement of Christ; the formal cause is God's justice, by which he makes us righteous and calls us to receive his righteousness.[1]

---

[1] In case this scholastic form of argument is unfamiliar to any reader, here is an analogy to bring out the senses of 'final', 'efficient', 'meri-

The Passion of Christ causes (still § 7) the charity of God to be poured into the impious heart (Romans v. 5). Faith cannot alone unite man perfectly with Christ or make him a living member of his body; hope and charity must be added. Faith without works is idle.

We are justified by faith (§ 8) because faith is the beginning of salvation and without that justification to which it leads we cannot please God. And this Justification is free. It must not be thought that either faith or works, preceding justification, are the means of procuring justification.

Now (§ 9) it is possible to place too much reliance on 'faith', and this can lead to a misplaced subjective confidence. It is not enough, as the heretics say, to believe one is justified. Therefore it is improper to speak of being justified by faith *alone*. How do the heretics imagine a man, *ex hypothesi* in a state of sin, can at that stage know he has saving faith?

The righteousness which is received at the moment of justification (§ 10) is increased by the process of sanctification. No justified man is exempt (§ 11) from keeping the Commandments. The doctrine 'by faith *alone*' can lead some men to pay too little respect to the Commandments.

At this point we may turn back to *A*.

A said that Justification is by faith alone. *T* denies the

---

torious', 'instrumental' and 'formal'. Suppose a boy is given a prize for good work at school. The *causes* of this event could be stated variously, including the following statements: He was given the prize (which was a book) in order to encourage him and promote an interest and industry he had already shown (*final cause*); he was given it because the Headmaster decided that he must have it (*efficient cause*); he was given it because he deserved it (*meritorious cause*); he was given it by the President of the Royal Society, who was the guest of honour at the speech day (*instrumental cause*); he was given it because it was the school's custom to give prizes for good work (*formal cause*). The fact that the cases are very far from parallel only emphasizes the evangelical precision of the Council's findings. For example, we receive Christ's benefits (*meritorious cause*) precisely not because we deserve them but because of the merits of Christ; the *instrument* of their reception is a divine, not a human, institution (baptism); the *formal cause* of the process is not a human system but a God-initiated one.

'*alone*'. The dispute turns on the meaning of 'faith'. As we have
already pointed out, *A* (IV) rests its argument on a solemn and
inclusive use of the word *credo*, which can only be translated
'wholly believe'. In *T* the argument turns on a lighter use of
the word, meaning simply 'think it probable'. *T*'s argument
in effect is: 'You may be wrong in your belief that you are
justified.' *A*'s argument is: 'Justification follows a total
commitment to the belief that Christ justifies you.' For *A* and
the Lutherans generally, this total commitment is *a priori*
assumed to be something altogether too fundamental to permit
of a subjective 'wrongness'. A man could not commit so much
to a belief if there were in his mind either hesitation or self-
deception (see above, p. 15).

In other matters *T* is as evangelical as *A*, and on its own
argument it is more so, since it virtually accuses *A* of Pelagian
teaching (the very last thing with which Luther would want to
be associated); it does so in ascribing to *A* a reliance on a human
belief which is not what it meant by 'faith'. But that a man is
justified by faith, and by the grace of God (faith being his
response, the grace of God being the cause), *T* leaves us in no
doubt.

T continues on *Predestination*, which is not a concern of *A*,
but which is a major concern of the Calvinist Confessions, and
of those Calvinists whose voices had already been heard in
controversy. Of Predestination, *T* (§ 12) simply says that
nobody ought to claim assurance that he is predestinated to
glory. The whole operation remains mysterious, and its results
are known only to God.

Here *T* would repudiate the assurance of glory which is
ascribed to the believer in the predestinarian Confessions.
Normally they say (see below, pp. 75, 88) that predestination
is of the elect, and that the elect knows he is predestinated to
glory, although he may make no judgment about others. *T* is
disinclined to go even as far as this.

The Christian (*T* continues, § 13) ought to persevere, though
he must not claim to be certain that his good works will bring

the reward of glory; the award is in the hands of God alone. Those who have sinned after Justification may (§ 14) be restored by the Sacrament of penance. Whereas *A* (XII) declares that sin will be forgiven on proof of contrition (detestation of the sin) and faith, *T* says that to contrition must be added the sacrament of penance, administered by a priest, which can include temporal punishment.

T holds (§ 15) that infidelity causes loss of faith as well as of grace, but mortal sin causes loss of grace but not of faith. Two possibilities are here implied: that of losing touch wholly with God's grace by the extinction of faith (i.e. by apostasy), and that of losing touch with it on account of sin. Both conditions are equally grievous, and result in an equal separation from God, and the distinction appears to be simply logical.

§ 16 deals with *Good Works* (and corresponds to *A* XX). Texts (of which 1 Cor. xv. 58 is one) are quoted to justify the doctrine that eternal life is promised to Christians who persevere in good works. But the goodness of our works is the consequence of the infusing into us of the virtue of Christ: or, to put it another way, of the imputation to us by God of his own righteousness. Our good works are therefore our duty, but the quality of righteousness, which makes them acceptable to God and efficacious towards eternal life, is not a quality of our own. Therefore a Christian must do good works but not glory in himself.

It is not easy to see how this differs radically from the extensive argument in *A* XX. *A* says (XX, § 14) that except our good works be under the Holy Spirit's direction they will not be good works at all. *T* says that their virtue is not ours but Christ's. *A* makes it somewhat clearer that it is arguing throughout in the dimensions of the converted life, dimensions which are unintelligible to the unregenerate life: but, after all, so is *T* arguing in those dimensions. But *T* is not ashamed, as Luther would have been, to attach 'merit', in this context, to good works.

The Canons (Session VI) analyse heresy in thirty-three

modes, to each of which anathema is attached. These heresies are those which say

1. That a man can be justified before God by his own works;
2. That grace is given that a man may *more easily* achieve Justification (implying that without grace he could manage it);
3. That Justification can come without the prevenient inspiration of the Holy Spirit;
4. That man's free will does not co-operate in preparing for Justification. (Note: *A* does not deny the will's co-operation; it denies that otherwise that under the Holy Spirit's influence it can co-operate. See *A* XVIII);
5. That Adam's fall extinguished man's free will, or made it unreal or illusory;
6. That God causes evil actions in man;
7. That all works done before Justification are sins;
8. That the fear of hell is a sin;
9. That justification of the ungodly is by faith alone (see *A* IV);
10. That men can be righteous without Christ's righteousness;
11. That men are justified by the righteousness of Christ alone, without the addition of the charity of the Holy Spirit;
12. That justification by faith is simply confidence in God's mercy (a repudiation of *sola fide*);
13. That for Justification a man must believe for certain and without hesitation or wavering that his sins are forgiven;
14. That a man is truly forgiven who believes that he is forgiven; and that he who does not wholly believe he is forgiven is not forgiven;
15. That a man who is regenerate must hold that he is predestinated to glory;
16. That a man once regenerate automatically receives the gist of perseverance;

17. That Justification is only attained by those who are predestined to glory;
18. That the commandments of God are impossible even for the regenerate to keep;
19. That the Gospel requires nothing besides faith; that other things are indifferent, neither commanded nor prohibited but free: and that the Ten Commandments are not binding on Christians;
20. That the justified man need not heed the commandments of God or the church, but is justified wholly by his belief alone;
21. That Christ is a redeemer in whom to trust, and not at all a lawgiver to obey;
22. That the justified man can persevere without the help of God; or without that help, cannot persevere;
23. That a man once justified cannot sin or lose grace: that therefore he who sins was never truly justified;
24. That the righteousness received is not preserved and increased through good works; and that the good works that follow Justification are simply its effect and not at all causes of its increase;
25. That the righteous man who does good works sins venially - or even mortally, and is only saved from damnation by the grace of God;
26. That the just ought not to expect eternal life as reward for good works;
27. That there is no mortal sin but apostasy;
28. That loss of grace means also loss of faith always; that the residual faith of a lapsed sinner is not a true faith; that faith without charity is not a quality of the Christian;
29. That he who has fallen after Baptism cannot rise again; or that he can rise without the sacrament of Penance;
30. That guilt is blotted out from a sinner's record without any consideration of temporal punishment;
31. That the justified who does good works with a view to eternal reward is a sinner;

D

32. That no merit attaches to the good works of a justified man;
33. That this doctrine of Justification is not for the greater glory of God.

These anathemas make it even clearer than the decrees that the chief disorder at which the Church of Rome is concerned to direct its attack is subjective anarchy in the Church. The closeness of so much of what is stated to what Luther preached and *A* taught, and of so much that is anathematized to what they anathematized, brings out the more strongly the deep cleavage at the point of 'faith', which *T* clearly regards as the source of all Reformed error, and *A* clearly regards as the source of all Roman error. In certain cases the teaching of *A* is milder than that of the Formula of Concord (see below, pp. 55-72); Canon 4, for example, does not radically contradict *A* XVIII, but it would contradict *FC* II. Reformed resistance to the spirit of Roman doctrine hardened at many points (and not only in consequence of the theological system of Calvin) into a more direct resistance to its letter. But apart from its explicit repudiation of *sola fide*, its rejection of Luther's interpretation of 'faith', and its insistence that human merit is not theological nonsense, *T* is more obviously an attack on Anabaptism and Antinomianism than on Luther and *A*. But in Tridentine doctrine 'faith' is a virtue of the intellect; for Luther, it is a quality of the whole person, which includes charity. At this point there is a deep cleavage between *T* and *A*. We shall soon proceed to show how the Calvinist Confessions in their turn make direct attack on *T*.

In its Seventh Session (3.3.47), the Council promulgated a brief decree and thirteen Canons concerning the *Sacraments* in general. These are (in précis) the Canons. They pronounce anathemas on those who teach

1. That the Sacraments are less than seven;
2. That the sacraments of the New Law do not differ from those of the Old;

3. That all are of equal worthiness (this will be explained in a moment);
4. That the New Testament sacraments are not necessary to salvation; that justifying grace can be obtained without them;
5. That they were instituted for the sake of nourishing faith alone;
6. That they do not contain the grace they signify (see below, p. 46);
7. That grace is not given through the sacraments always and to all, though some receive them wrongly;
8. That the grace is not conferred *ex opere operato*;
9. That the sacraments of Baptism, Confirmation and Order (i.e. Ministry, and Ordination) there is not 'imprinted on the soul a character, or sign, so certain and indelible that they cannot be repeated';
10. That all Christians have the right to administer the Word and the Sacraments;
11. That in a minister who dispenses the Sacraments there is not required at least the intention of doing what the Church does;
12. That even mortal sin in a minister takes away from the efficacy of the Sacrament;
13. That the approved rites of the Church may at any time be set aside and others substituted at any pastor's will.

These Canons declare implacable controversy with Reformed doctrine as it is implied in *A* and expounded in the Calvinist Confessions. The implication of Canon 3 is that Martin Luther is wrong in holding that *all Sacraments* are of equal worthiness because *all are of the Word of God*. There is no Roman doctrine of the relative worth of the Sacraments; but it was regarded as pernicious doctrine to ascribe all their worthiness to the Word of God and none to the Church. Canon 8 expressly reaffirms what *A* XIII denied. Canon 9 is directed rather against Anabaptist doctrines of the necessity of re-baptism, and Canon 10 against Anabaptist anti-clericalism. Canon 11 recalls a hyperbolic interpretation of Luther's 'justification by faith', namely, that even if the sacrament were administered as a joke or a mockery, it would be valid. It was not here intended to discuss the question whether the moral standing of the priest affected the validity of the Sacrament. Luther and the Catholics agreed in any case that it did not (and the Calvinist Confessions say the same).[1] It was, as a matter of fact, a question debated in the Council and not fully agreed, whether mockery invalidated the Sacrament. One Catharinus held and defended the opinion, after the close of the Council, that provided the celebration was decent and reverent outwardly, the intention of the priest at this point made no difference to its validity. But this was not the Council's view.

Once again, the Council is determined to make an end of the mischief which it believes that the Lutheran doctrine of 'justification by faith alone' is causing.

This is even more evident in the Canons concerning *Baptism*, which incorporate the following doctrines:

1. The baptism of John had not the same force as that of Christ.
2. True and natural water is necessary for baptism.
3. The Roman Church holds the true doctrine of baptism.
4. None the less, baptism administered by heretics may be valid.
5. Baptism is necessary to salvation.
6. After baptism is it possible to lose grace otherwise than by apostasy.
7. The baptized is obliged not only to faith but to the whole law of Christ.
8. The baptized is obliged to all the precepts of the Church.
9. Baptism does not make all vows taken after baptism irrelevant.

[1] Luther's doctrine about the moral standing of the priest will be found near the end of the first section ('On the Lord's Supper') of his *Babylonish Captivity* (1520). See B. Lee-Woolf, *Reformation Writings of Martin Luther*, Vol. I (1952), p. 253.

10. Baptism does not bring with it automatic remission of sins, or make mortal sins venial.

11. If a man be baptized, and lapse from the faith, and later return, he is not to be baptized again.

12. Baptism is not to be administered only at the age at which Christ was baptized.

13. Children, having been baptized, are to be counted among believers, and are not to be rebaptized at maturity.

14. If a person having been baptized as a child refuses to confirm the vows taken on his behalf, the Church must by all means persuade him to do so, and exclusion from the Eucharist is not the only means of persuasion open to the Church.

Paragraph IX of *A* is extremely conservative on Baptism, saying no more (apart from a condemnation of the Anabaptists) than that 'it is necessary to salvation, and by Baptism the grace of God is offered, and that children are to be baptized, who by Baptism being offered to God are received into God's favour'. There is no direct contradiction of this in the Canons. But there is abundant contradiction of Luther's teaching in the *Babylonish Captivity*, especially at three cardinal points.

Canon 1 may be compared with this in Luther: 'It is wrong to hold that the sacraments of the New Law differ from those of the Old Law in point of their effective significance: both have the same meaning, for the God who now saves by baptism and the Supper, saved Abel by his sacrifice . . . Abraham by circumcision. . . .'[1]

Canon 6 directly opposes this in Luther: 'See how rich a Christian is, that is, one who has been baptized. Even if he wishes, he could not lose his salvation however often he sinned, save only if he refused to believe.'[2] Canon 10 also points in the same direction.

Canon 9 may be compared with the whole teaching of Luther in the same document, that compared with the vows taken at Baptism and the faith implied in them, all vows taken by a

[1] Lee-Woolf, *op. cit.*, p. 262.   [2] *Ibid.*, p. 257.

Christian after baptism (especially monastic vows) are of secondary, and indeed of trifling importance.[1]

Canon 5 does not oppose the letter of *A*, but it opposes the spirit of Luther's teaching, and the explicit teaching of the Calvinist Confessions. Canon 7 similarly is directed at the heart of the doctrine of 'justification by faith alone'.

On the *Eucharist*, the Council's findings were published from its Thirteenth Session, in a Decree of eight chapters followed by eleven Canons. Here follows a summary of the Decree:

§ 1. 'After the consecration of the bread and wine, our Lord Jesus Christ is truly, really and substantially contained under the species of those sensible things' (*vere, realiter ac substantialiter sub specie . . . contineri*).

§ 2. The Sacrament was instituted as a remembrance of his work, and as a spiritual nourishment, and as an antidote by which we may be 'freed from daily faults and preserved from mortal sins'.

§ 3. Since this Sacrament alone *contains* the Lord, it is unique among Sacraments and superior to the others. 'The others have the power of sanctifying when one uses them: in the Eucharist, before it is used, the Author of sanctity himself is present.' (*Note:* this is what was implied in Canon 3 on the Sacraments.)

§ 4. 'By the consecration of the bread and the wine, a conversion is made (*conversionem fieri*) of the whole substance of the bread into the substance of the body of Christ our Lord, and of the whole substance of the wine into the substance of His blood; which conversion is by the holy Catholic Church suitably and properly called Transubstantiation.'

§ 5. The Sacrament may be worshipped and venerated both in and outside the Church.

§ 6. It may be reserved and carried to the sick.

§ 7. Sacramental Confession is the correct form of preparation for receiving this Sacrament, both on the part of the laity and of the celebrants.

---

[1] Lee-Woolf, *op. cit.*, p. 273 ff.

§ 8. There are three ways of receiving the Sacrament:

- (a) *Sacramentally*—as it is received by sinners;
- (b) *Spiritually*—as it is received by those who look for heavenly nourishment;
- (c) *Sacramentally and Spiritually*—as it is received by those who receive it spiritually but, knowing that they are sinners, have prepared themselves beforehand. The third mode is therefore the most to be desired.

Canons (Session VII):

1. In the Eucharist are contained truly, really and substantially the body and blood together with the soul and divinity of Christ: it is error to reduce this by saying that He is figuratively or virtually present, or present 'by sign'.[1]
2. There is a conversion of the whole substance of the Elements, not a conjunction of Christ with them.
3. The whole Christ is contained under each species and under every part of each species.
4. The whole Christ is and remains in the Elements, and therefore they may be reserved: His presence is not confined to the moment when they are actually being taken after consecration.
5. The effects of the Sacrament may not be confined to the remission of sins.
6. Veneration of the Sacrament therefore is not to be forbidden.
7. Reservation is not to be forbidden.
8. Christ is eaten not spiritually only, but also sacramentally and really.
9. All of years of discretion are bound to communicate at least every year at Easter.
10. The celebrating priest must communicate himself.

[1] In these three adverbs are condemned respectively the doctrines of Luther, Calvin and Zwingli.

11. Faith alone is insufficient for the proper use of the Sacrament; Sacramental Confession must be added.

This was the Council's final reply to the 'ten heads of doctrine' which, taken from the teaching of those whom it now condemned, had been before it since January 1547. There is scarcely a single detail in which it meets the Reformed teaching. It is hardly necessary to particularize, since all the main points here raised will appear in the Calvinist Confessions, which produce their own answers to the enormous questions raised first by Zwingli, Luther and Calvin and then, with varying emphases and dogmatic contortions, in the Eucharistic Controversy of 1549-74 (see below, p. 58). All depends here on the doctrine of Transubstantiation, which is simply stated in §§ 1-4 of the Decree, without any scholastic argument. From that proceed naturally the veneration of the Sacrament and its reservation.

The Roman contentions are pressed home, however, in later decrees of the Council. In Session XXI (16.7.62), the Council decrees that nobody is obliged to receive the Sacrament in both kinds. The arguments for this are stated to be (1) that the emphasis in St. John vi. 52 ff. is always on the 'flesh' and the 'bread', even though the 'blood' is also mentioned; (2) that the Church has power to change 'what things soever it may judge most expedient for the profit of those who receive ... the said Sacraments'; and (3) that in any case Christ is wholly and entirely present in either species of the Sacrament. These arguments, together with a decree that small children are not required to take Communion, are set out in four chapters and four canons.

The question of Communion in both kinds is not raised in *A*, but Luther makes a firm point of it in the *Babylonish Captivity*, near the beginning,[1] where he pours special scorn on argument (2) above. It is, of course, the consensus of the Calvinist Confessions that Communion must be offered in both kinds. None of the Reformers is impressed with that 'tradition' and

[1] Lee-Woolf, *op. cit.*, pp. 217-224.

'custom' which Rome holds to have good reason behind it. (If the reason for withholding the Cup was in the beginning one of simply hygiene, it is an attitude characteristic of the Reformers to regard faith as more powerful than the fear of infection.)

Matters concerning the Eucharist are further and finally decreed in Session XXII (17.9.62), under the general head of *the Sacrifice of the Mass*.

Here the doctrine, in nine chapters of Decrees and eleven Canons, is as follows:

§ 1. The historic sacrifice of Christ on the Cross was made once for all. But in the institution of the Eucharist Jesus offered to God his own body and blood under the species of bread and wine; the Mass is therefore instituted to be a visible sacrifice which will *represent* (present again, not merely be a symbol of) the bloody sacrifice once offered.

§ 2. This sacrifice is of propitiation both for the living and for the dead. The efficacy of the bloodless sacrifice for the forgiveness of sins does not derogate from that of the bloody sacrifice once offered.

§ 3. Where masses are offered in honour of saints, they are not an offering of sacrifice to them, but to the God who crowned them.

§ 4. The Canon of the Mass is to be implicitly observed.

§ 5. The solemn ceremonies of the Mass are instituted for the help of human nature, which requires such help.

§ 6. Where at Mass the priest alone communicates, the people are deemed to communicate spiritually; the Mass is celebrated by the priest not for himself alone but for all the faithful.

§ 7. For the mixing of water with the wine there is Scriptural precedent (John xix. 34).

§ 8. It is better for the mysteries of the Mass to be celebrated everywhere in one language, and explained to the people, than to be celebrated in the vernacular.

The Canons, introduced by § 9 of the Decree, cover the same ground, instituting anathemas on those who do not hold these doctrines. Then there follow (breaking the normal pattern of these documents) Decrees concerning the things to be observed and avoided in the Celebration of the Mass. These are:

(1) That covetousness be avoided, all payments for 'new' masses are prohibited (*novis missis*: a difficult phrase which may mean either first masses for young people or masses newly appointed), and all 'importunate and illiberal demands, rather than requests, for alms'.

(2) That irreverence be avoided, the Mass should not be celebrated by any unknown priest, or any priest who is known to be a criminal or evil liver. Nor should it be celebrated otherwise than in churches or oratories designated by those who have authority to do so. Music of a secular or 'lascivious' kind is to be banished, and also all 'profane conversations, all walking about, noise and clamour'.

(3) That superstition be avoided, the Church's rites must be preserved and not altered, Mass shall be observed only at the appointed hours, and such customs as the use of candles and the celebration of a fixed number of masses shall be prohibited. The people are to be instructed properly, and encouraged to frequent Communion.

Here then, at last, the Council, having established its dogmatic position uncompromisingly, seeks to meet the complaints of the Reformers concerning the abuses prevalent in the Church. While Indulgences and payments for masses are not forbidden, they are strictly limited. A series of puritan clauses seeks to purge the Mass of irrelevant accretions. The power of local pastors to alter the Church's rites is denied, and that of the Ordinaries is, by implication, strictly limited.

At last the intentions of the Council towards Reformation are made clear. Their respect for dogma is to be clearly stated, and their faith in the Church's authority is unabated. Provided this is established, those things which are clearly abuses are to be reformed. Within this Decree can be seen the Roman Church's answer to (and substantial agreement with) several sections of the second Part of *A*: for example, §§ 4-5 on money,

§§ 8-10 on the multiplication of masses and, within dogmatic
limits, §§ 15-40 on the power of the bishops to institute
ceremonies.

Other matters can now be dealt with quite briefly.

On the *Marriage of Priests*, the Council answers Reformed
complaints (such as that expressed in *A* II ii) in Canon 9 on
Marriage (Session XXIV, 11.11.62), declaring that the Church's
law forbids the marriage of priests, but does not thereby
condemn marriage. This is part of a long passage on Marriage,
which is declared to be a Sacrament, and in respect of whose
solemnization many detailed regulations are laid down.
(Luther's teaching and argument are to be found in his *Appeal
to the Nobility*, 1520, § 14).[1]

On *Penance, Confession and Satisfaction*, *A* II iv argues that
Confession, an excellent practice, has become corrupted
through the obscuring of the primacy of faith by the imposition
of satisfactions (temporal punishments). The Council in
Session XIV (25.11.51) declared its mind. Against *A* it main-
tains that enumeration of sins is essential in Confession (§ 5),
and that a sin committed after baptism must be followed by
satisfaction if its forgiveness by God is to be assured (§ 8); it is
argued that this is precisely the difference between him who
sins before baptism and him who sins after it, that he who has
been baptized is in a more serious condition when he sins, and
without the prospect of satisfaction may come to believe that
baptism has removed the possibility of sinning, or anyhow of
sinning mortally. On this cf. Session VII, Canon 10 (p. 45
above).

Luther's teaching on this matter is in § 3 of the *Babylonish
Captivity*; a special point that he makes concerning 'reservation'
of Confession (that is, the custom of appointing that certain
grievous sins be confessed not to the parish priest but to a
superior)—a practice whose corruption he especially deplores,
is met in § VII of the Council's Decree. This enacts that especially grievous sins can receive absolution (except in cases of

[1] Lee-Woolf, *op, cit.*, pp. 158 ff.

imminent death) at the hands only of superior priests. Luther's main contention is, however, that the whole practice obscures the operation of God's forgiveness. The Canons insist that Confession is a Sacrament, and that Penance and Satisfaction are Sacraments; that the absolution of the priest is a judicial as well as a spiritual act (Canon 9), and that confession in private prayer is in no circumstances sufficient to procure the Church's absolution and with it the forgiveness of God.

The complaint of *A* II vi concerning *Monastic Vows* received very careful attention in Session XXV (4.12.62), which published a long Decree of twenty-two chapters on the subject. In the fifteenth of these it is provided that profession of men or women for monastic vows shall not be accepted before the age of sixteen, or except after a year's probation; and in chapter 18 it is declared that any kind of compulsion on a woman to enter a convent and undertake the religious life is rigidly forbidden. It is implicitly admitted in the other chapters, by their rigorous provisions for the regulation of religious communities, that much required to be repaired in their manner of life and control; the particular effect of the Council was to remove a large measure of the autonomy which these communities had enjoyed and place them under the examination either of a Bishop or of a Superior priest (§§ 11, 20).

At the end of the proceedings of this Session XXV there are decrees on Indulgences and Fast Days. That on *Fast Days* gives the Church authority to appoint fasts and feasts and the choice of meats. Exception was taken to this whole system in *A* II v as being an impediment to faith and a needless exaltation of works. Luther's own views on the matter are set down at the end of § 19 of his *Address to the Nobility*.[1] No concessions are made by the Council to his objections.

On *Indulgences*, on the other hand, while the Council decrees that they are legitimate and a necessary consequence of the doctrine of purgatory, it adds, 'being desirous that the abuses which have crept therein, and by occasion of which this

[1] Lee-Woolf, *op. cit.*, p 168.

honourable name of Indulgences is blasphemed by heretics, be amended and corrected, the Council ordains . . . that all evil gains for the obtaining thereof—whence a most prolific cause of abuses among the Christian people has been derived—be wholly abolished'. It further enjoins on all bishops the duty of scrutinizing the practice concerning Indulgences in their own districts, that all that is of 'superstition, ignorance, or irreverence' may be rooted out.

Throughout the Sessions of the Council a series of 'Decrees of Reformation' was drawn up, alongside the decrees and Canons of doctrine. These were not of the reformation of doctrine, but rather of the reformation of the Church's discipline and practice. In themselves they form the Council's answer to the kind of objections raised at great length in *A* II vii. They concern the limitations of authority, the administration of all branches of the Church, the increase of holiness among the clergy, and the check of ignorance and incompetence among them. Taken together they provide the most notable of all the Council's concessions to the body of opinion which informed the Reformation. They need not here be examined in detail.

It may be judged then that the Council of Trent, in its twenty-five Sessions spread over eighteen turbulent years, showed by no means an uncompromising face to the Reformed criticisms. Wherever it was possible to disentangle a practical abuse from a disputed doctrine, the amendment of the abuse was directed by the Council. But wherever a Reformed objection, either in the writings of Luther or in *A*, associated a complaint with the doctrine of justification by faith alone, the Council rigidly insisted on the condemnation of the doctrine, and therefore the irrelevance of the complaint.

By the time the Council was over (early 1563), Calvinist doctrine was fully codified, and was opposing the spirit and the letter of Roman doctrine with an intellectual rigour that contrasts strongly with, and formidably supplements, both the religious rhetoric of Luther and the conservative but significant demands of *A*. The Council was too late by forty years with its concessions, and to the now hardened second-generation opinion of Reformed Europe appeared merely a reactionary gesture. Its consequences in the Church of Rome, through the Counter-Reformation, were profound and in places revolutionary; but these appeared to the heirs of the Reformation to substitute a reformed and streamlined and efficient and less blameworthy Rome for the corrupt and indulgent Rome they had attacked: and they liked it none the better for taking to heart even so much of their criticism as it had done. The breach between Rome and the Reformed Churches was now beyond any reconciliation, and it was to be three centuries before even the gesture of the Oxford Movement in England was to offer the least question to the axiomatic enmity between the two. The additions and modifications to the doctrines of the Council of Trent made between that day and this are of such small moment as to make it unnecessary for us to repeat, in this study of Confessions, this incursion into orthodox Catholic doctrine. From now onwards we must be concerned with Reformed and Protestant doctrine. The chapter of ecumenical reconciliation between Rome and Reformation cannot yet be written, but the suggestion that it could be written is at least not now merely utopian. The Adiaphoristic Controversy (see below, pp. 61-2) indicated that many even in those days were prepared under pressure to see how far they could go by way of compromise with Rome. The Oxford Movement separated many things that were permanent from many that are impermanent in the controversy between Rome and the Church of England. Of those things which are in sharp dispute between T and A, only the dogma of transubstantiation, the practical matter of the marriage of priests, and the vitally important question of the interpretation of 'faith' remain matters of high contention today. And notwithstanding the addition to these of certain political and dogmatic points of controversy—in particular, that of the nature of the Church, with which neither T nor A deal in any detail—it is impossible to think that reconciliation could at no time be achieved without contradiction of conscience on either side.

IV.—THE FORMULA OF CONCORD, 1576-84[1]

THE *Formula of Concord* was originally written in German 1576, and published at Dresden, 1580. The first Latin translation by Osiander, 1580, was found defective and revised by two of its original authors, Selnecker (1582) and Chemnitz (1583); the authentic Latin edition was published at Leipzig, 1584.

The *Formula* was an attempt to re-draft the Lutheran Protestant Faith after a series of controversies which had occupied the theologians during the years separating it from the Augsburg Confession (1530-76). These were:

(i) The continuing controversy between Luther himself and Melanchthon, the author of the Augsburg Confession. Of the two men, Schaff writes[2] that while Luther in his later years 'had so strongly committed himself and was so firm in his convictions, that he was averse to all further changes and compromises', Melanchthon, 'with less genius but more learning, with less force but more elasticity, with less intuition but more logic and system than Luther, and with a most delicate and conscientious regard for truth and peace, yet free from the weakness of both a compromising and temporizing disposition, continued to progress in theology, and modified his views on two points—the freedom of the will and the presence of Christ in the Eucharist; exchanging his Augustinianism for Synergism, and relaxing his Lutheranism in favour of Calvinism'. On Free Will *A* had said that while human free will undoubtedly exists, it is able to exercise judgment only in affairs of this world, and not at all able to exercise it in matters pertaining to man's relation with God. *A* left it there, but Melanchthon grew dissatisfied with the Augustinian position there implied as it affected the matter of Conversion. For this

[1] See P. Schaff, *Creeds of the Evangelical Protestant Churches*, pp. 93-180; *History of the Creeds of Christendom*, pp. 258-340.
[2] *HCC*, pp. 260-1.

he substituted the doctrine that the human will co-operates with the divine action in effecting conversion. He protected himself from the charge of Pelagianism by saying that the primary cause of conversion is the Holy Spirit, and the secondary 'instrument' the Word of God (in Scripture), and that the human will merely co-operated, presumably having freely decided to co-operate. His opponents gave this teaching the name of *Synergism*. With this Luther found himself in total disagreement.

As to the Lord's Supper, Melanchthon found himself unable to accept Luther's literal interpretation of the Words of Institution, and his teaching that in receiving the elements one literally 'eats' the body and 'drinks' the blood of Christ. He never had agreed with Luther that the body of Christ could be everywhere (the doctrine of 'ubiquity', i.e. that wherever Bread and Wine were consecrated, there were in literal fact the body and blood of Christ); he held that this teaching violated the essential doctrine of Christ's Ascension. This was a matter upon which *A* did not specifically touch.

Indeed, it was possible to interpret the Augsburg Confession as agreeable to either side on both these points. Hence arose a controversy between parties which were called respectively Lutherans (Jonas, Amsdorf and later Chemnitz, Selnecker, Andreae and Chytraeus) and Philippists (among whom were Bugenhagen, Eber and Pfeffinger, who influenced especially the religious opinions at the universities of Wittemberg and Leipzig). All claimed to be 'Confessional', and all held implicitly the authority of the Bible. On interpretation at these two points they differed.

(ii) The Flacian Controversy on Original Sin. This controversy, between Matthias Flacius (1520-75) and Victorinus Strigel (1524-69), turned on the question whether Original Sin was essential or accidental: whether it was inseparable from man's nature or a corruption of his nature. Flacius taught that it was essential and inseparable. He did not hold that physical nature was essentially corrupt, but only that moral nature was essentially corrupt; hence he could not be accused of

Manicheanism. But he was regarded as heretical and deposed from his chair of N.T. at Jena.

(iii) The Synergistic Controversy. This was the revival of the controversy referred to under (i) above, but in the second generation. It was opened by Pfeffinger, a Professor at Leipzig, who restated the synergistic view in an academic treatise in 1550, and subsequently (1555) wrote a book on the Freedom of the Will. Major, Eber, and Crell of Wittemberg and Strigel of Jena followed him. Flacius, Amsdorf, Wigand and Heshusius opposed him.

(iv) The Osiandric Controversy. Andrew Osiander (1498-1552), Professor at Königsberg, had the temerity to seek a modification of the Lutheran doctrine of justification by faith. Where Luther pressed the forensic note in the metaphor— man justified before God as a criminal might be justified before his judge by the intercession of his advocate—Osiander interpreted justification as an 'infusion of the divine nature of Christ'. This sounded, to the Lutherans, mystical and Romish and out of key with the Reformation. Controversy was so bitter in Königsberg that it is reported that the professors for a while carried their guns into their classrooms. Osiander died in 1552, but his part in the controversy was taken by John Funck, his son-in-law, who in 1566 was executed as a heretic and a disturber of the peace.

Two minor controversies were associated with that of Osiander: that initiated by Francesco Stancaro (d. 1574), also a Professor at Königsberg, who made the theological point that Christ was our Mediator according to his human nature only (since in virtue of his divine nature he could not mediate: *nemo potest esse mediator sui ipsius*); and that associated with the name of Georg Karg (1512-76), who derived our redemption solely from Christ's passive obedience.

(v) The Majoristic Controversy, in which Georg Major (d. 1574), a Professor at Wittemberg, asserted that good works are necessary to salvation. He was denounced as teaching popish doctrines, especially by Amsdorf and Flacius.

(vi) The Antinomian Controversy. This was an early phase

E

of a dispute which proved unusually intractable in Protestant circles, and which appears again in the history of English Puritanism. Antinomianism is the condition that results from excessive emphasis on the replacement of 'law' by 'grace', and in its extreme form teaches that nothing which was enjoined on men before Christ (or which is binding on the consciences of men who are not Christians) is binding on Christians. Luther's doctrine had been balanced at this point. For him, repentance consisted of knowledge of sin and sorrow for it, which was the effect of the work of 'law', and resolution towards amendment of life, which came of 'grace'. John Agricola of Eisleben (1492-1566) began to teach that law had nothing to do with the Christian case at all, and that therefore it need not be taught. That meant in effect the total severance of Christian experience from any natural conscience, or sense of right and wrong. The Augsburg Confession had spoken of the Gospel as the comfort of the *conscientia perterrefacta*; and implied that the 'terror' was implanted by 'the law' (we know we have done wrong: we know we are not reconciled to God: and we do not know why this is or how it is to be handled). Agricola's teaching was virtually quietism—nothing could be done until the grace of God did the double work of terrifying the conscience and consoling it. This matter is to some extent cleared up in the Formula of Concord.

(vii) The Eucharistic Controversy (sometimes called the 'crypto-Calvinistic' Controversy). This was the backwash of the dispute between the views of Melanchthon and Luther referred to above. It lay between those who followed, or thought they followed, either of the principal Reformers. A leader of the 'Lutheran' view was Joachim Westphal, who in 1552 and succeeding years denounced as heretics all who did not hold the literal and corporeal presence of Christ in the Sacrament. Calvin himself joined in the dispute, and claimed to agree with Melanchthon, who however had shot his bolt by then and declined to be involved further. But it was Calvin's intervention that caused German-speaking followers of Melanchthon to be called 'crypto-Calvinists'. All over Germany this became a burning issue, and scenes of violence were enacted even in churches (in Heidelberg Tilemann Heshusius attempted to snatch the Cup from the hands of the officiating pastor, Klebitz, in defence of the 'high' Lutheran doctrine). At the popular level, wild superstition followed in the wake of the disputes, fantasy taking the place of speculation. The learned argued whether the eating of a crumb of sanctified Bread would or would not kill a mouse; a local minister in Rostock required all his communicants to be shaved, on the ground that licking the 'blood' from the beard would be punished with death or a monstrous growth. Further, there was argument on the question whether the Lord was corporeally present only during the time of the use of the Elements at the service of Holy Communion, or for all time after they were consecrated. There was much wisdom in the remark of Chytraeus that these were questions of 'idle curiosity rather than piety'.

(viii) The *Ubiquitarian Controversy* was closely associated with the Sacramental controversy in gathering itself round the implied 'ubiquity' of Christ's Body and Blood. Obviously, if Christ was corporeally present wherever the Bread was blessed, he must be present here and there and yonder at the same time. The question then was, Is he present in his divine nature or in his human nature, or in both? Appeal was at once made to the patristic doctrine of *communicatio idiomatum* or *perichoresis*, which defined the limits within which it could be intelligibly said that the quality of one nature was shared by another (or that the attributes of one Person of the Trinity could be ascribed also to the others).

Luther's doctrine[1] had included the ubiquity of Christ's Body, and he based it on Eph. i. 23, 'The church . . . which is his body', and John iii. 13, 'The Son of man . . . which is in heaven'. Driven to amplify this, he argued in effect that everything depends on what is meant by 'in' in the sentence 'Christ is in the bread'. Is He in it as water is *in* a cup ('local' presence)? Or is He in it as the soul is *in* the body ('definitive' presence—a somewhat misleading expression, the point being that the

[1] In his *Grosse Bekenntnis von Abendmahl* (1528).

precise discernment of soul and body is impossible?) Or is He in it as He is in heaven ('repletive' presence)? (This last is not well illustrated in Luther's somewhat circular argument. The 'in' here is presumably the 'in' of the whiteness 'in' a lump of chalk or of the sweetness 'in' a lump of sugar. A cup can be empty of water; a body can be without a soul, when it is a corpse; sugar cannot be without sweetness, or heaven without Christ).

Having asked the three questions, he concludes that the answer to all three is 'yes'. And in doing so he is driven by logic to say more than his later writings show he could have seriously meant. But it was enough to support those who took an extreme ubiquitarian view a generation later.

The question was successively dealt with at the Colloquy of Maulbronn (1564), which was inconclusive, the Consensus of Dresden (1571), which favoured the Philippists, and, long after the publication of the Formula, in the Tübingen and Giessen Controversy on Kenosis (1616-25). Martin Chemnitz (1522-68) was the most successful of the mediators in the dispute, and his doctrines were more or less written into the Formula. In effect he argued that while even in glory, after the Ascension, Christ's body is *somewhere*, he may choose to be present where he will, and can be believed to be present in that Sacrament which is of his institution.[1]

---

[1] In the course of his argument Chemnitz happens to mention Stephen's sight of Christ as he was about to die by stoning (Acts vii. 58). There is a strange and illuminating echo of this, in an imaginative and strictly pastoral context, in a sermon of Alexander Whyte's on Stephen, which contains this passage:

'Behold', he exclaimed with the stones crashing about his head. 'I see the Son of Man standing on the right hand of God!' But the Son of Man does not now any more stand, surely. For when He had by Himself purged our sins He surely sat down for ever on the right hand of God. 'Sit, said the Lord to my Lord, at My right hand until I make Thy foes Thy footstool.' But with all that, He could not sit still when He saw them stoning Stephen. And so it is with Him always. He sits, or He stands, or He comes down to earth again, just according to our need, and just according to our faith. I see him standing up, says Stephen. What a power, what a possession, is faith!

That may be sacred rhetoric, but it is pure Chemnitz.

(ix) The Hades Controversy. This turned on the question whether, when we say in the Creed, 'he descended into Hell', we mean that Christ (a) suffered a local change, and literally went down to a place where the lost have their abode, and (b) suffered the 'pains of hell' as part of his act of redemption. Luther had preached graphically of Christ's descent into hell and his triumphant progress against the devil (at Torgau, 1533). Later John Aepinus of Hamburg began to base much teaching on a literal application of this poetry. Melanchthon, appealed to, was characteristically cautious, and discouraged violent dispute on matters not clearly revealed in Scripture, but on the whole thought it best to follow Luther, provided the doctrine was a 'harrowing of hell' rather than anything resembling the undergoing of punishment for sin.

(x) The Controversy of Compromise (1548-55). This is classically and terrifyingly called the Interimistic or Adiaphoristic Controversy. It was the direct consequence of the Schmalkald war, which brought the Lutheran states under the control of the Roman advisers of Charles V. The Augsburg Confession had said that diversity of usages could co-exist in the Church with agreement and unity in doctrine. Could this clause be invoked to justify the reintroduction of Romish rites in places where under the Reformation they had been abolished, or to comfort the consciences of those who were forced to reintroduce them? In the southern states (where Roman Catholicism still prevailed) Lutheran pastors were dismissed, under the Augsburg Interim (1548) for non-conformity. In the same year the Leipzig Interim, enacted by the Elector Maurice, with the advice of certain Lutheran divines including Melanchthon, required conformity to the Romish ritual (including episcopal ordination and most of the Canon of the Mass, with many ceremonies, fasts, processions and the permission of images) but preserved essentially the evangelical Creed, including the vital clause concerning justification through faith by the sole merits of Christ.

Melanchthon advised conformity with these compromises, and his advice seemed to many to betray the Reformation.

Flacius, fleeing from Wittemberg to the free city of Magdeburg, instituted open war with Melanchthon and his 'compromisers' (adiaphorists). The troubles were ended only with the breach between the Emperor and Maurice, the defeat of the Emperor by Maurice, and the ensuing Peace of Augsburg (1555).

(xi) The Predestination Controversy (1561-3). The doctrine of Predestination could be analysed, by reference to the three emphases respectively of Luther and Melanchthon, Zwingli and Calvin, into the concepts of *servum arbitrium*, *providentia* and *praedestinatio*. Melanchthon, of course, later deserted the full doctrine of *servum arbitrium*, but it was characteristic of Luther that his doctrine should make predestination the consequence of a proposition about the human will, and equally characteristic of Calvin that for him it was a consequence of the absolute sovereignty of God.

Dispute about this flared up at Strasbourg, between Jerome Zanchi (1516-90) and John Marbach (1521-81), respectively Professor of Theology and Superintendent of the Church. Zanchi, following the teaching of his predecessor, Martin Bucer, taught the Augsburg Confession with a Calvinistic accent. He was opposed to the 'ubiquity' doctrine, and taught the acceptance of Christ in the Eucharist not as a corporeal acceptance but as acceptance by faith. Upon predestination he said (1) that the elect receive from God the gift of true saving faith only once, (2) that faith once received can never be finally lost, for the promises of God and the intercession of Christ are both more powerful than our sin (for example: when Peter denied Christ, faith was not lost in his heart) and (3) when a man sins, he sins not with his whole heart and will, but sins in the external man against the internal man.[1]

From this followed a form of predestination, or election, which depended on faith and demanded the perseverance of the believer. Once elected to the state of grace, a man could not wholly fall away from it; therefore he was predestined to

---

[1] There is a striking parallel to this sentiment in the words of a modern interpreter, W. B. J. Martin, 'Sin is any action which cannot be consented to by the whole person.'

glory. Marbach's opposition appears to have been entirely personal and temperamental. He sought to teach the opposite of everything that Zanchi taught, and considerable personal ability and command of rhetoric advanced his claims at the expense of the theologically more deserving ones of Zanchi. Among the points of dispute was, therefore, that of predestination, which was taken up by the doctors of Marburg, Zürich and Heidelberg, who favoured Zanchi's position, and those of Saxony, some of whom favoured Zanchi on the Eucharist but rejected him on predestination, while the others registered favour and disfavour the opposite way. Temporary peace was made by Zanchi's accepting a compromise in the Strasbourg Formula of Concord (1563) and promptly leaving for Italy.

But the stage was now set for the preparation of the Formula of Concord of 1577-84, which was designed to make peace in a Church which sorely needed it. The architects of the formula were Augustus, Elector of Saxony (1533-88), who paid the expenses, Jacob Andreae (1528-90), who spent much energy in travel and negotiation, Martin Chemnitz (1522-86) and Nicolas Selnecker (1539-92), theologian and hymn-writer, who between them compiled the first draft.

The *Formula of Concord* is a document some 17,000 words in length divided into twelve long articles, each of which is subdivided into two main sections headed *Affirmativa* and *Negativa*. We shall here extract from it only those passages which positively bear on the Augsburg Confession and the subsequent controversies.

The Formula opens with an *Epitome* of the articles, which summarizes the purpose of the Formula and, as it were, opens its concluding speech. It declares that 'the one rule according to which all dogmas and teachers are to be judged, is the prophetic and apostolic Scriptures of the Old and New Testaments'. No other writing, patristic or modern, can claim the authority of the Holy Spirit. It further judges (§ 3) that the 'first, unaltered Augsburg Confession of 1530' is authoritative for the whole Reformed Church. The laity can be safely guided by the Shorter and Longer Catechisms of Martin Luther. There follow the twelve articles.

Article I. *Of Original Sin* (see Controversy (ii) above). Is Original Sin an inseparable property of human nature, or a corruption of it? It is a corruption only, because God not only created the body and soul of Adam and Eve before the Fall, but has continued to create our bodies and souls since: and God cannot create evil. Moreover, the Son of God has assumed our nature, yet without sin, and sanctifies and glorifies it in the Resurrection. We must therefore distinguish between *corruptam naturam* and *corruptionem quae natura infixa est*. Not but what this corruption is 'so profound as to leave nothing healthy, nothing uncorrupt, in man's soul or body'. Only God can separate this corruption from our nature: but it is heresy to teach that even God cannot do this.

Article II. *Of Free Will* (see Controversy (i) above). Can man in any way prepare himself by the use of his native faculties to receive the grace of God? The answer is that man's understanding and reason are *in spiritual matters* entirely blind. His unregenerate will is not only averse from God but also hostile to Him. The only human agency that is used by the Holy Spirit towards conversion is the preaching of the Word. But (Neg. § 1) the Formula repudiates all determinism as being a Manichean error, and the unexplained teaching that the will of man is before, during and even after conversion opposed to the Holy Spirit (Neg. § 8). Accepting Luther's doctrine that the will in conversion is passive, it insists that after conversion the will is indeed free; and that in any case these limitations on the freedom of the will are confined to the 'spiritual' world—the area of discourse in which conversion and regeneration move. They have nothing to do with the day-by-day decisions that men have to make concerning the things of this world.

Article III. *Of the Righteousness of Faith before God* (see Controversy (iv) above). Is Christ our Mediator according to his divine nature, or according to his human nature, or according to his whole nature? The answer is—according to his whole nature. Justification and the forgiveness of our sins are the same thing (Aff. § 5, cf. Neg. § 3). They are achieved for us by Christ precisely in virtue of the combination in him of divine and human nature. His obedience (Aff. § 4) is essential to this achievement. Our own works have nothing to do with it (Aff. § 7). The power to redeem is in his divine nature, the obedience by which he redeemed is in his human nature (Aff. § 1).

Article IV. *Of Good Works* (see Controversy (v) above). If it be said that good works are necessary to salvation, in what sense can this be true? Answer—'necessary' is essentially an unhappy word to use, and we avoid it. Controversy arose (preamble §§ 1-2) because some have said that good works are necessary to salvation. This is true only in the sense (Aff. § 1) that good works necessarily follow from the condition of being saved. It is not true in the sense that good works help us to be saved (Aff. § 2). However—confusion arises from the word 'necessary'. Some have argued (preamble § 2) that no good work is 'necessary' because except it be 'free' or 'voluntary' it is not a good work. Others again argue that our obedience, resulting in good works, is not a matter of free will, and therefore the good works follow the state of salvation of necessity, not only logically but morally.

So we say this: that while the state of grace gives rise to good works, the condition of a saved man (Aff. § 3) is that they are 'obliged' to good works (*debitores ad bona opera facienda*). In that sense 'necessary' is permissible (§ 4), but (§ 5) not in the sense of constraint. We must distinguish between a mechanical constraint and a voluntary obedience. When we say that good works come spontaneously from a saved man (§ 6) we do not mean that he is free to do good or ill, but (§ 7) that a saved man does good works from the love of righteousness, and not as a slave who fears punishment for doing ill. (In modern terms: he welcomes his duty.[1])

---

[1] The reader who wants a modern exposition of this vital principle in Reformed doctrine may care to turn to my book, *The Gift of Conversion* (1957), where it is expanded in chapter 6 and chapter 9, § 5.

Article V. *Of Law and Gospel*; Article VI. *Of the Third Meaning of 'Law'* (Article VI is directed against Controversy (vi) above: Article V prepares the way for it). Is the preaching of the Gospel a proclamation of grace only, or should it contain a rebuke for the sin of unbelief? The answer is that it is a dangerous practice to preach with the primary emphasis on rebuke of sin (Neg.). The Gospel preaches repentance: but it must never preach it as it would be enjoined under the law. It must always (Aff. § 7) be so preached that 'men may at last see how much God requires of us in his Law, and how utterly unable we are to meet his requirement except in Christ'. In other words, we must not so preach as to leave the impression that (*a*) this and that is wrong, and (*b*) by doing this and that we can set it right. But (proceeding to Article VI) it is a great error to suppose that the regenerate have no need of hearing and obeying the Law. We must distinguish between 'The Law' as a condition of life in which good works are done through fear of punishment, which is not the way the regenerate live (Aff. § 4), and Law as the revealed Will of God, unchangeable and perfect (§ 6). The regenerate man does the Will of God freely and spontaneously (§ 5), but he needs to be told, by the Holy Spirit working through preaching and through daily and nightly meditation (§ 1), what the Will of God is.

Article VII. *Of the Lord's Supper* (see Controversy (vii) above). In what sense is Christ present in the bread and the wine at the Lord's Supper? The answer is that He is 'truly and substantially present' (*vere et substantialiter*, Aff. § 1), as the New Testament testifies (§ 2). This is due not to the effectual working of the words of institution (§ 3), but to the omnipotence of Christ. The Words of Institution are to be recited at Communion (§ 4).[1] The body and blood of Christ are taken at Communion 'not only spiritually through faith, but with the mouth (*non tantum spiritualiter per fidem, sed etiam ore,* § 6); yet they are received, *non*

[1] Note that the scriptural words here required are 1 Cor. x. 16, not 1 Cor. xi. 23 ff.

*Capernaitice, sed supernaturali et coelesti modo, ratione sacra-
mentalis unionis*.[1]

When the unbelieving receive the Sacrament (§ 7) they too
receive truly the body and blood—but to their condemnation.
The unworthy guests (§ 8) are those who do not believe, not
those who are sinners (we are all sinners). And our belief
consists in Christ's obedience and perfect merit, applied to
ourselves by true faith (§ 8).

Therefore (Neg. § 1) transubstantiation in the Romish form
is rejected, because it teaches that the substance of the bread
and wine is changed while its accidents remain. It suggests the
annihilation of the substance. For this the Formula substitutes
a conjunction of the body and blood of Christ by faith. It
insists, however (Neg. § 5) that it is an error to teach that the
body of Christ is received by faith and the bread by mouth.
This is to destroy the true conjunction. The 'manducation'
(eating) of the Body and Blood (Neg. § 21) is 'true but supernatural' (*vera sed supernaturalis*), not 'Capernaitic'.

Article VIII. *Of the Person of Christ* (cf. Controversy (vii)
above). In what sense are the divine and human natures in
Christ in communication? The answer is complicated. The
divine and human natures in Christ are personally united
(Aff. § 1). There are not two Christs, one human and one
divine, but one, who being Son of God became Son of man.
Each nature (§ 2) retains its own attributes; they are not
mingled with one another. Therefore (§ 3) the attributes of the
divine nature are omnipotence, eternity, infinity, and the
capacity to be omnipresent; these cannot be or ever become
attributes of the human nature. Similarly the attributes of
the human nature (§ 4) are corporeality and creatureliness,
flesh and blood, finitude and the capacity for suffering, death,

---

[1] This phrase is designed to guard against gross materialism. The body
and blood are taken *with* the bread and wine (*cum pane et vino*), not *in*
them. 'Capernaitice', an untranslateable word (Schaff says 'Capernaitic-
ally') is 'shorthand' for the attitude of crude materialism which in
John vi. 27 ff. and 52 ff. was assumed to have misled the people of
Capernaum concerning our Lord's teaching on the 'eating of his flesh'
and 'drinking of his blood'.

descent, ascent, moving from place to place, hunger and thirst, and all kinds of physical feeling and affliction. These neither are nor can become attributes of the divine nature. The union of the natures (§ 5) does not imply the interchange of these attributes, in such wise that the divine nature could (for example) suffer or be thirsty, or that the human nature could be omnipotent or omnipresent. But this is not to say that there is no communication between the two natures. True, it is not as if 'two boards were glued together—neither giving anything to the other or affecting the other'—just attached by the glue. It is not so because the two parties to the union are not things but personal natures, and they communicate as persons communicate, neither swamping the other or detracting from each other's essence, but none the less each giving to the other. It is, as the fathers said, like fire in glowing iron, or like body and soul.[1] This is why we are able without error to speak humanly of God (e.g. in calling him Father), and equally to speak of Christ as one with God. It is therefore permissible (§ 7) to speak of Mary as the Mother of God. Nothing that Christ did was done by a 'mere man' (§ 8) for us men, but by God in man. The Son of God suffered (§ 9), but in his human nature; and through this suffering was raised, in virtue of his divine nature, to be our High Priest. Similarly (§ 10) we can say that the Son of Man is truly exalted to God's right hand.

The Incarnation (§ 11) was a humiliation, and a putting off (*exinanitio*) of the divine majesty. Until after his resurrection he only made use of his divine power when he saw fit; the use of it was not normal. But, risen, he set aside the 'form of a servant', but not the human nature. Therefore we can speak of our High Priest's compassion, since 'not only as God, but also as man, he now knows everything, can do everything, is present everywhere, and has under his feet everything which

---

[1] An analogy more familiar to modern eyes is, of course, the glow of the filament in an electric light bulb; and indeed it is a better analogy, because iron is only heated in order that it may be changed in shape; whereas it is an essential part of the filament's action that it be filled with fire.

is on the earth, above it, or under it'. Among these attributes of his resurrected human nature is the capacity to be present (§ 12) in the bread and the wine.

Among the errors enumerated in the twenty negative articles, those of Nestorius, Eutyches, Arius and Marcion are rehearsed, together with modern variations of Christological error, and finally it is insisted (§ 20) that Christ in his incarnate years was not bereft of his divine power. The power was with him, but (cf. § 11) he renounced it voluntarily as part of his 'humiliation'. This renunciation was not absolute, and in his 'signs' the power was made visible.

Article IX. *Of the Descent into Hades* (cf. Controversy (ix) above). In what sense are we to understand that Christ descended into Hades? The authority for a right interpretation is Luther's Torgau sermon of 1533—that Christ 'harrowed hell' in triumph. The doctrine should not be disputed about, in default of scriptural explicitness, but should be taught as simply as possible, with Luther's emphasis.

Article X. *Of Ceremonies* (cf. Controversy (x) above). Is it possible with a good conscience to observe ceremonies which the Reformers have done away if in an emergency they are reimposed by the enemies of the Reformation, seeing that ceremonies are of human ordinance and therefore scripturally indifferent? The answer is that such ceremonies and rites as are not expressly enjoined in Scripture are not divine worship. Therefore it is open to the Church to change such customs at any time in any locality. But (§ 3) occasions of offence, whether by omission or commission, are to be avoided. This (§ 4) may well make it a matter of principle to resist any imposition of ceremonies by our enemies, especially where they reimpose what has been done away because it gave offence. Ceremonies and customs (§ 5) are not to be an occasion of one Church condemning another.

Article XI. *Of Eternal Predestination and of God's Election.* (This is not, as might be expected, designed to a settlement of Controversy (xi) above. It is claimed in the preamble that 'there has arisen no public controversy among the theologians

of the Augsburg Confession' on this matter.) God's foreknowledge must be distinguished (§ 1) from his predestination and
election. Foreknowledge extends to all things (§§ 2-3), but is
not the cause of sin, or the cause why men perish. Predestination, on the other hand (§ 4), extends only to the 'good and
beloved children of God'. It is fully revealed (§ 5) in the Word
of God. Predestination then must be regarded as God's
direction of the good (§§ 6-10) to eternal life, or as Christ's
calling of them to eternal life, and is a matter of great consolation. Men direct *themselves* (§§ 2 and 11) to eternal death, and
this is against God's will and design. It is only through faith
in Christ (§ 12) that men can avail themselves of this predestination; but this does not release men from the duty (§ 13) of
persevering in goodness. The notion that some are predestined
to perdition is expressly declared an error in Neg. § 3.

FC^1 thus seems to hold side by side the doctrines of the
helplessness of the sinner, and of his duty to persevere towards a
state of grace (compare II, § 2, with XI, § 13). *A* had no
article specifically upon Predestination. It was Calvin and his
followers who argued with ruthless logic on this matter.
Luther's emphasis had always been on the divine grace and
vocation. The nearest he comes to speaking of predestination
to perdition (which doctrine is an error according to *FC*) is
when he writes in his Commentary on Romans of 'resignation
to hell'.[2] But this means not God's direction of the soul to
perdition, but man's acceptance of the whole judgment of
God, his loving acceptance of a judgment which may consign
him, and has the right to consign him, or part of him, to
perdition.

In arguing of Predestination it is necessary somehow to
provide for God's sovereignty and yet to provide against God's
creation of evil. Some were led to say that since God foreknows
all things, he knows who will go to perdition and who will go
to felicity; if this knowledge be equated with God's will, then
it must be his will that some shall go to perdition. Therefore it

---

[1] Formula of Concord: so from here on.
[2] See E. G. Rupp, *The Righteousness of God* (1953), p. 189.

is a righteous will that sends them there, and the sending them there is not an evil act. But if the will is separated from the foreknowledge, as it is in *FC*, then the fact that some go to perdition cannot in any way be held against God. He knows that they will go, and he knows who will go, but it is through their wilful opposition to his will (the will to save them) that they go.

The Lutheran emphasis, preserved in *FC* Article XI, is that man has no *right* to heaven, and no means within himself of achieving it. That is another way of saying what is said in Article II, that he is totally depraved. In coming down on the side of single predestination alone, *FC* preserves the idea that predestination is simply of the saved, and that in connexion with the rest the matter does not arise. This is attractive, though hardly logical. That comment it answers by discouraging enquiry (Neg. preamble) into mysteries. So, for his part, does Calvin. *FC* further protects itself against the notion that God predestines man to particular evil acts which will lead to perdition by (§ 3) separating predestination from foreknowledge. All determinism has already been anathematized (II Neg. § 1).

It is only in the matter of *perseverance* (which *was* the main point of Controversy (xi) above) that *FC* shows an inconsistency that cannot be covered by an appeal to mystery. There indeed *FC* has told us at one point that man is helpless and at another that man can persevere. But in Article II the Augustinian severity was relaxed at one point—the efficacy of the preaching of the Gospel. What Article XI omits is any reference to this, which might have bridged the gap.

It is therefore true, as Schaff says, that *FC* is inconsistent, but it is possible that he overemphasizes the inconsistency[1] by attending too little to the overriding conviction of Luther and his followers that positive argument could proceed with reference to God's grace and its operation, while speculation as to what happened when that operation was frustrated, or even as to the sense in which it could ever be said to be

[1] Schaff, *HCC*, pp. 314 and 330.

frustrated, was in the end vain.[1] By its silence on the specific point, *A* endorses this attitude.

Article XII is a general condemnation of all who do not hold the Augsburg Confession, specifically mentioning the Anabaptists, the Schwenkfeldians (followers of Caspar Schwenkfeld, 1490-1561, who opposed the doctrine of justification by faith and held an heretical position concerning the 'deified humanity' of Christ), the new Arians, and the Anti-Trinitarians. These controversies are not within the field of this present study.

Perhaps the *Formula* is chiefly to be criticized in that (no doubt because it was an attempt to settle so many controversies) it leaves the impression of trying to define too much that cannot be defined. The word 'Concord' in its title suggests that it is, in a modified way, an ecumenical document. Its contents warn those who engage in ecumenical movements of reconciliation that it is not in definitions, and especially not in defining that concerning which certainty is denied to finite minds, that the way to unity essentially lies. The same conclusion, of course, was reached by Cyprian in *De Unitate* (see above, p. 5).

[1] See, for example, Luther, *Table Talk*, 66: *Commentary on Romans* at 8. 31 ff.

V.—THE SECOND HELVETIC CONFESSION, 1566

THE Second Helvetic Confession is so called to distinguish it from the First Helvetic Confession (1536), which is itself alternatively named the Second Confession of Basel (Basiliensis). (The First Confession of Basel is dated 1534.) Basel II or 1H[1] is a short document published in German and Latin, and running some 3,000 words in twenty-eight articles. Among its authors was Henry Bullinger of Zürich, who was the sole author of 2H[2]. Since 2H was of wider authority than either of its predecessors[3] and is more lengthy and detailed (it runs some 20,000 words), we pass over the others and attend to it here.

It is in thirty articles, of which many add nothing significant to the Reformed doctrines that have already been discussed under the German documents. But here for the first time we hear the voice of that Protestantism which is familiar in Britain and America.

Article I confesses belief in the Scriptures as the Word of God, and Article II declares that the Fathers and the Councils and Traditions of the Church are of high, but secondary, authority. Article III declares the Trinitarian faith and denounces all anti-Trinitarian heresies; Article IV denounces all image-worship, and declares that the image of Christ should not be tolerated in church. Article V asserts that adoration and invocation must be directed to God only through Christ, and not therefore through the saints, whom it is right to honour, but not to worship.

---

[1] First Helvetic Confession.

[2] Second Helvetic Confession; so from here on.

[3] 2H held authority in the Swiss Cantons and the Palatinate, and in the Reformed Churches of Neufchatel (1568), Basel, France (1571), Hungary (1567), Poland (1571) and Scotland (1566). It was translated into Dutch, Magyar, Polish, Italian, Arabic and Turkish, as well as German, French, and English.

F

Article VI handles the question of God's Providence. God (§ 1) rules and sustains all things in heaven and earth and (§ 3) cares for them.

(§ 4) *Interim vero media, per quae operatur divina providentia, non aspernamur ut inutilia, sed his hactenus nos accommodandos esse docemus, quatenus in verbo Dei nobis commendantur. Unde illorum voces temerarias improbamus, qui dicunt: si providentia Dei omnia geruntur, inutiles certe sunt conatus nostri et studia nostra.*

That is, the Confession does not hold that all human effort is vain, but, on the contrary, that God uses secondary causes for the operation of his providence, and these are discernible in Scripture.

Article VII declares that God created all things, and that those are in error who believe that one deity created what is good, another what is evil (the Manichean-Gnostic error). The devil (§ 3) is an angel who 'was a liar from the beginning'. (It is implied that God created him.) Man (§ 6) consists of soul and body. The body is mortal, the soul immortal, but (§ 7) the soul is not a part of God.

Article VIII affirms the doctrine of original sin. Sin is (§ 2) *nativa illa hominis corruptio*—that native corruption in men whose consequence is our proneness to evil and our aversion from good. When Scripture says (§ 9) that God hardens men's hearts or blinds them, this is a way of expressing God's judgment on men already in sin. God does not make a man evil, but he permits him to be evil by his own choice. To the question (§ 10) whether Adam fell by God's will, there is no answer.

Article IX. *On Free Will*, says that the Lutheran doctrine, incorporated in *FC*, that man is like a stick or a stone, is too harsh. The sinner is a sinner by his own will, not under compulsion. Three conditions are distinguished. (1) Before the fall, man was free to do good or to do evil. (2) After the fall, and before regeneration, man's understanding is darkened, and his will is enslaved to sin: his will is still a will, but it tends towards sin. (3) Regeneration brings true freedom, in which the mind is enlightened that it may understand the will of God (§ 7), and the will is not only 'changed by the Spirit, but instructed in its faculties, that it may of its own accord wish for and be capable of the good' (Rom. viii. 5-6) (*voluntas ipsa non tantum mutatur per Spiritum, sed etiam instruitur facultatibus, ut sponte velit et possit bonum*).

Article X, *Of Predestination and the Election of the Saints*, asserts (1) (§§ 1-3) God has undoubtedly predestined some people to glory, and these, being believers, know it, but (2) (§§ 4-6) it is misleading to insist that only a few are predestined; it is right to hope for eventual election for all men; and it is wrong for any man to ask whether and to what he is elected (§ 7), (3) The preaching of the Gospel is our guide, and faith is our only means of approach, to the truth about Election, and the doctrine of Predestination (§§ 8-9) is designed to be a comfort to hesitant believers. There is no teaching in the Confession concerning predestination to perdition.

Article XI summarizes at length the orthodox teaching concerning Christology, that Christ is very God and verily Man, and the sole Saviour of the world. Concerning the divine and human nature it follows the *A* (III) and *FC*. Concerning the final Judgment (§ 13) it follows *A* (XVII). Articles XII (*Of the Law of God*) and XIII (*Of the Gospel of Jesus Christ*) follow the accepted Reformed teaching. stating that the Law is our teacher concerning sin (for saved as for unsaved), and that the Gospel is the good news concerning salvation and regeneration. It insists that this (XIII, §§ 4-7) is not new doctrine, but that it is implied in God's whole plan from the beginning of the world.

Article XIV, *Of Penitence and Conversion*, states the plain doctrine that Repentance is a change of heart, and that the confession of sin to God in public worship or in private prayer is sufficient as an act of penitence, without recourse to priestly confession (§ 6). The 'Power of the Keys' (§ 8) is given 'to all ministers lawfully called' who exercise it in the preaching of the Gospel and in the administering of the Church's discipline, but not through private confession or profitable indulgences.

Article XV teaches of justification *sola fide in Christum, non lege, aut ullis operibus* (§ 4). Article XVI endorses the Augustan teaching concerning 'Good Works', insisting (§ 8) that they are not to be despised or called useless, but (§ 5) that the only significant kind of 'Good work' are those which proceed from a 'living faith' (*ex viva fide*).

Article XVII teaches *Of the Holy Catholic Church* and the *Sole Head of the Church*. Its chief heads of belief are these:

1 (§ 1). 'Since it was God's will from the beginning that men should be saved and come to the recognition of the truth, it must follow that there always has been, now is, and will be to the end of time, a Church: that is, a congregation of the faithful called or gathered out of the world; this congregation is a fellowship of all the saints, that is, of those who truly know God in Christ the Saviour through the Word and the Holy Spirit, and rightly worship him. These participate in all the benefits freely offered by Christ'.

2 (§ 2). There is one universal Church, dispersed throughout the world, ruled by one God and saved by one Saviour. Within the Church there are human varieties, and the Church militant on earth and that triumphant in heaven are in communion with one another.

3 (§ 4). This Church, so long as it rests on the authority of the Apostles and Prophets, is infallible (*non errat*). It needs no Vicar of Christ (§ 5) because that implies Christ's absence. Christ is its *immediate* Head. The Church is a spiritual 'body of Christ' (§ 6) and Christ's Headship is similarly spiritual. Similarly, Christ is the Church's *immediate* Priest (§ 8) and therefore the Church needs no human Supreme Pontiff.

4 (§ 13). Without Christ (or 'outside' Christ: *extra Christum*) there is no salvation: that is our position vis-à-vis those who say we offend against the Patristic doctrine that without the Church there is no salvation (*extra ecclesiam nulla salus*).

5 (§§ 14-16). The Church is *invisible* in the sense that the true number of believers is known only to God. It is an error to attempt to assess it. The presence of imperfect Christians in the Church is a fact of human life that must be borne with by men.

6 (§ 17). The true unity of the Church is rather to be sought and found in the truth and the Catholic faith than in external ceremonies and rites. The Catholic faith is handed down to us in holy Scripture and summarized in the 'Apostles' Creed'. Ceremonies may vary, but unity, which all Christians must cherish, lies in obedience to the Apostolic faith.

(The paragraphs in this article not explicitly mentioned here contain matter which confirms these doctrines by scriptural proof, or which answers objections, or which denounces heresies that are held to disagree with the faith here declared.)

Article XVIII is concerned with *The Ministry*. The lawful offices in the Church are those which were constituted by the Apostles (§ 5)—the names of these offices being Apostles, Prophets, Evangelists, Bishops, Presbyters, Pastors and Doctors (or Teachers). (The terms are explained: Bishops are *inspectores vigilesque Ecclesiae, qui victum et necessaria ecclesiae dispensant*—overseers of the Church, who dispense its nourishment and necessities. Of these the contemporary Church can now be content with Bishops, Presbyters, Pastors and Doctors —i.e. overseers, elders, shepherds of the flock of Christ, and men of learning.)

The monastic orders (§ 7), while they have served a purpose in the past, were not instituted by the Lord or by the Apostles, and have since fallen into corruption.

Ministers hold office (§ 8) in virtue of their legitimate call of the Church. They must be elected by the Church in a true religious spirit (or by the Church's appointed officers), without any contention or faction. They must be men of learning, eloquence and prudence. Ministers are not priests (§ 11), because Christ alone is our eternal priest. They are 'dispensers of the divine mysteries' (*oeconomos vel dispensatores mysteriorum Dei*, § 12). All ministers carry equal authority (§ 16), and none can be set over his fellows demanding obedience from them. The Bishop and the Presbyter were originally the same, and episcopal authority can only be interpreted in terms of service. Their duty is to preach the Word, administer the Sacraments and care for the flock of God (§ 18). The efficacy of Word or

Sacraments does not depend on the moral character of the minister (§ 21), but (§ 20) it is proper that the Church should have courts of discipline properly constituted to watch over the conduct of ministers. It is lawful (§ 23) for the minister to be maintained by his congregation.

Article XIX. *Of the Sacraments*, argues under these main heads:

(1) The Papists count seven sacraments: the Protestants count two; as the Old Testament enjoined two 'sacraments', circumcision and the Paschal Lamb, so the New Testament enjoins baptism and the Lord's Supper. Of the other so-called Sacraments, Protestants acknowledge repentance (*poenitentia*), ordination and marriage as 'useful institutions', and altogether reject Confirmation and Extreme Unction (§§ 1-2).

2. Sacraments are instituted wholly by God, and not at all by men. This is the case both in the Old Israel and in the New. The Sacraments of the Old Israel hold the promise of Christ the Saviour: those of the New attain the substance of this promise (§§ 3-7).

3. Sacraments, in both dispensations, consist in the word, the sign and the thing signified (*verbo, signo, et re significata*). That is, they are instituted by the Word of God (the command in Scripture), they employ a *sign* (water: bread and wine), and they signify eternal reality (§ 8).

4. The signs are not changed into the things signified (§ 9). They are set aside for special use; they carry with them a special meaning and benefit; they can be referred to as 'the washing of regeneration' or 'the body and blood of Christ'; indeed, as Sacraments, they must not be received merely according to their outward form (i.e. baptism is not mere washing, but a special kind of washing: and Communion is not mere eating and drinking but a special kind of eating and drinking). But for all that, no change is held to take place in the Elements. The mystical meanings are *attached* to them (*conjunguntur*), not effective of a change in them (§§ 9-13).

Article XX, *Of Baptism*:

1. Baptism is of Christ's institution (§ 1).

2. 'There is one baptism only in the Church of God, and it is sufficient to be baptized once as an initiation into God. Once undergone, baptism lasts for life, and is a perpetual seal of our adoption. To be baptized in the name of Christ is to be inscribed, initiated and received into the covenant, the family, and the inheritance of the sons of God, to be named by God's name, that is, to be called a child of God; and it is to be washed from the stains of our sins, and given the various gifts of God that lead to a new and innocent life' (§ 2 verbatim).

3. We were all born in sin, children of wrath. Baptism is the washing away of the stain of sin and the refreshment of the wrath-oppressed soul (§ 3).

4. Baptism separates us from other religions and peoples, and consecrates us a 'peculiar' people of God. By it we are enrolled in Christ's army under the oath of our faith, to fight against the world, the devil and the lusts of the flesh (*contra mundum, Satanan, carnem propriam*). And we are baptized into one body of the Church, consenting with all the members of the Church in one and the same religion and in mutual service.

5. Baptism must be administered by ministers of the Church, not by women or by nurses. It is an office of the Church. It is an error to teach that it may not be administered to children, because it is the teaching of the Gospel that children inherit the Kingdom of heaven and are within the Covenant of grace (§§ 5-6).

Article XXI. *Of the Lord's Supper:*

1. The Lord's Supper, or Eucharist, instituted by Christ, is a grateful remembrance of the benefits which Christ gained for us, and a constant renewal of that remembrance (§§ 1-2. 'Remembrance', of course, in the N.T. and Latin sense of 'bringing into present consciousness', not in the modern sense of 'projecting ourselves into the past') (§§ 1-3).

2. There are three ways in which the elements of the Communion could be eaten: in two of these ways they are in fact eaten.

(i) *Manducatio corporalis*—the reception of food into the

mouth, its mastication by the teeth, and its digestion in the
stomach. This is not the means by which the Sacrament is
received, and to say that it is is to perpetuate the Capernaitic
error. We do not say that the flesh of Christ is literally eaten
(§ 4).

(ii) *Manducatio spiritualis*—the spiritual reception of the
body and blood of Christ, which brings with it our liberation
from death and the forgiveness of our sins (§ 5).

(iii) *Manducatio sacramentalis*—by which the believer not
only inwardly receives the body and the blood but outwardly
receives them at the Lord's table through the seals of the
Communion (§ 8).

These categories are only logically separable, not practically.
The teaching is that the believer 'receives' the body and the
blood at the Communion 'spiritually' and 'sacramentally',
distinguishing two things which in the Lord's Supper always
happen at the same time. The purpose of the analysis is to
stress the equal necessity of belief in the inward effect of the
Sacrament, and of faithful practice of its outward obligations.
It is not sufficient to hold that any bread or wine consecrated
by pious words at any time can be the body and blood of Christ
to the believer: they must be consecrated by the Church and
by its ministers at a Eucharistic service; but conversely it is
not sufficient that they be so consecrated, if there is not faith
in the believer. (§ 9). The inward and the outward are comple-
mentary and equally necessary to salvation. It is important,
however, to make clear that *manducatio corporealis*, with its
implications of transubstantiation, has nothing to do with the
case (§ 10).

3. Though the body of Christ is absent, being in heaven with
the Father in consequence of the Ascension (§ 8), none the less
the Lord is present with his people through faith.

4. The Supper increases our consciousness of membership of
Christ and of one another (§ 11).

5. Unnecessary complexities such as have gathered round
the Mass (§§ 12-13) are undesirable, and the withdrawal of the
Cup from the people is an especial abomination.

Article XXII, *Of Public Worship*, enjoins upon all believers the duty of public worship, without withdrawing their privilege of private Bible-reading and prayer. Ministers and pious magistrates should urge people to attend worship, and decent and convenient but not sumptuous places should be provided for it. It should contain the preaching of the Word, and should be wholly conducted in the vernacular tongue (§§ 1-4).

Article XXIII enjoins the subject of public prayer (for the rulers of the world, for the Church, and for any special need of the world, § 1), their style (*sponte, non coacte, neque pro ullo pretio*: free, not by prescription nor for payment, § 2), and their length (*ne nimis sint prolixae et molestae:* avoiding a vexatious prolixity). Singing is convenient but not compulsory (§ 4), and no hour of the day need be regarded as more suitable than any other for public worship (§ 5).

Article XXIV makes regulations concerning *Feasts, Fasts and the Choice of Food*. The days on which Christians make special celebration are the Lord's Days, which Christians observe not 'with Jewish superstition' but as a day set aside for worship and rest (§§ 1-2).[1] It says that the celebration of the Nativity, the Circumcision, the Crucifixion, the Resurrection and the Ascension of Christ, and of Pentecost, are wholly to be approved (§ 3); but that man-instituted feasts in honour of saints are rejected. Public fasts should be observed in times when the Church is in special need (§ 5), but they should come from a willing mind and be cheerfully assented to, and not be a matter of bondage (§ 6). The fast of Lent cannot Scripturally be imposed on believers (§ 7).

Article XXV deals with the Catechism of the Young and the Visiting of the sick; Article XXVI with the burial of believers, care for the dead, the doctrine of Purgatory and the appearance of Spirits. It enjoins the simple burial of believers, without superstition, and forbids prayers for the faithful, who may be assumed to have gone straight to heaven (§§ 1-3);

[1] There is a certain wry humanity in the last sentence of § 1: '*Nisi otium iustum concedatur religionis externae exercitio, abstrahuntur certe ab eo negotiis suis homines.*'

it rejects the doctrine of purgatory (§ 4) and also all manner of necromancy and spiritualism (§ 5). Article XXVII repeats the familiar Reformed doctrine of Ceremonies, stating that Ceremonies were, like all things under the law, the 'instructors' of the old Israel, but must not by any means be imposed on Christians. Article XXVIII makes certain injunctions about Church Property and its use and disposition.

Article XXIX, *Concerning Celibacy and Marriage*, declares that marriage is instituted of God (§ 2), denounces polygamy and incest, requires parental consent in all cases, and provides for the celebration of marriage with a religious service. The Church is given control of marriage-guidance and is required to arbitrate in matrimonial disputes. It is the parents' business to educate children in the fear of God (§ 3) and in the precepts of godly living. These duties (§ 4) which are a part of the marriage-duty are no less important and pleasing to God than prayer, fasting or almsgiving. Any opinion which prohibits marriage or tends to devalue it is denounced.

Celibacy is approved for those who are called to it (§ 1). Those who are so called are more fitted for the care of sacred matters than those who are distracted by family concerns: but those who have not the gift of celibacy may recall the Apostle's words in 1 Cor. vii (Marriage is therefore implicitly not forbidden to ministers). Celibacy of the unclean sort (§ 5) is of course wholly disapproved.

Article XXX deals with the authority of the Magistrate, holding that magistracy is appointed for the preservation of the world's peace by God, and among his duties are the protection of religion and the punishment of heretics (provided they are clearly proved to be so) (§ 3). War (§ 4) is permitted in self-defence, and only after the exhaustion of all attempts to preserve peace. It is not forbidden to Christians to hold public office.

As may well be expected, the teaching of the Helvetic Confession stands very close to that of John Calvin. There are certain points at which it will probably be useful to bring out the matters of agreement and disagreement between the emphases of the two treatises.

1. *On Predestination.* The 1*H* (1536) had no direct reference to Predestination; on Original Sin and Free Will its teaching is amplified in 2*H*. Calvin's developed teaching in the last edition of the Institutes provides for predestination both to bliss and to perdition (as does that of St. Thomas Aquinas) (see *Inst.* III 21-25). Much depends, in dispute about this doctrine, on whether one holds, with Calvin, that 'God's will cannot be distinguished from God's permission' (III 23, 8). If that be the case, double predestination is the necessary consequence. Those who hold that Predestination is to be predicated only of the elect must hold that God 'permits' but does not 'will' the perdition of the reprobate. This is the implied position of 2*H* (Article X). It shows a disagreement with Calvin's full doctrine, but on the other hand it follows to the letter Calvin's earlier doctrine, as it is expressed in the 1539 and 1541 editions of the *Institutes* and in the 1537 *Instruction in Faith* (§ 13). Indeed 2*H* X 9 at the beginning uses Calvin's very words (from 1539 and 1541), 'Christ is the mirror in which we can contemplate our predestination). Calvin and 2*H* agree (and so do all the expositors of this doctrine) that sooner or later one runs into mystery before which human reasoning is helpless. Calvin's earlier teaching and that of 2*H* place that point this side of reprobation; Calvin's later teaching beyond it. Calvin always insists, however, that the identity of the reprobate is known to no earthly eyes (III 23, 5), and he holds that the persever-ance of the elect is part of his duty under the protection of Christ (III 24, 6-10).

2. *The Church.* Whereas 2*H* XVII 4 teaches that the Church is infallible provided that its authority rests on the Apostles and Prophets, Calvin prefers to say that the Church is not infallible (*Inst.* IV 8, 12), but that what authority it has rests on its conformity with Scripture, and is correlative to its obedience to it. This difference of emphasis is the consequence of Calvin's graver preoccupation with controversy with Rome. It is not really a large point of difference.

(b) 2*H* XVII 14-16 teaches that the Church is *invisible*, in
the sense that its membership is known only to God. Calvin
prefers (IV 1, 2 at end) to say that the Church is 'hidden', and
uses the word to cover two ideas—that its membership is
known only to God, and also that at some times its work in the
world may be hidden through persecution, but must not be
thought ever to be extinguished. He also distinguishes the
visible from the invisible (II 1, 7) by referring on the one hand
to those who are the elect, and whose names are known only
to God, and on the other to the visible and imperfect Church,
in which many 'ambitious, greedy and envious persons' are to
be found. 'Just as we are bidden to believe that the invisible
Church is known to God, so we are bidden to revere and keep
communion with the visible'. This teaching is repeated in 2*H*.

(c) *On the Sacraments*. The teaching of 2*H* is thoroughly
Calvinistic here, and 2*H* XIX-XXI may be compared with
Inst. IV 14-16. Concerning the relation between faith and the
validity of the Sacraments, Calvin teaches (among other more
familiar doctrines) that the Holy Spirit works in us to persuade,
and to kindle in us a teachable mind, so that we may accept
the gifts of Christ not blindly, as when one man hears another
trying to persuade him by argument but cannot feel in himself
any answering assent because he has no confidence in the
authority or conviction of his persuader, but rather willingly,
as when the persuader's arguments are reinforced by his own
personal integrity and conviction (IV 14, 10). *A fortiori* all this
must be true of the Holy Spirit.

The Word must, says Calvin, explain the sign (IV 14, 4), and
the *sign* must be distinguished from the *matter* (IV 14, 15) in
the Sacrament. Calvin's philosophical and Biblical approach
to the relation between sign and matter is replaced by the
doctrine of the three senses of *manducatio* in 2*H* XXI 4-8,
which is clearly an attempt to go as far as can honestly be
gone to meet the more mystical opinions of the Lutherans.

(d) *Baptism*. The teaching against emergency baptism at
the end of 2*H* (XX 6) is there grounded on Paul's injunction
against women's bearing office in the Church. In Calvin

(IV 15, 20) it is grounded in the denial that Baptism *per se* is necessary to salvation, and that those who die unbaptized are consigned to limbo or perdition (IV 16, 26). There is no teaching in 2*H* on the question whether Baptism is necessary to salvation. Infant baptism is approved in both; 2*H* 6 approves it by the implication of the condemnation of Anabaptism, *Inst*. IV 16 develops a long Scriptural defence of infant baptism which 2*H* summarizes in a sentence—'For according to the teaching of the Gospels, theirs is the Kingdom of heaven and they are within God's covenant; why then should they not be given the sign of the Covenant?'

(e) *The Lord's Supper*. Calvin's argument against Transubstantiation is set forth in IV 17, 14. The heart of his argument is that Transubstantiation weakens the true purpose of a Sacrament. If bread is changed so that it is no longer real bread but, as it were, delusive bread, something which is not what it appears to be, the believer is being deceived by God. It is a much more powerful incitement to the adventure of faith if the elementary substance of bread, unchanged, is held to *signify* the body of Christ than if it is supposed by the operation of a miracle to become, and then literally to *be* that Body. The whole dynamic of faith is encouraged by the juxtaposition of the eternal and the real, but it is lamentably extinguished by the replacement of the real by the eternal. This argument lies behind what is written in 2*H* XXI 4-8.

That Christ is really present to the believer, and that this is a necessary consequence of the doctrine of the Ascension, is taught by Calvin (IV 17, 19 & 27) and firmly endorsed in 2*H* XXI 8. Similarly the doctrine of 'ubiquity' is rejected by both (cf. 2*H* XXI 4 with *Inst*. IV 17, 31). Calvin is more explicit than 2*H* in demanding that the Word be always preached when the Sacrament is administered (IV 17, 43), and the two agree with all Reformed statements that the Cup should not be withheld from the people (2*H* XXI 12; cf. *Inst*. IV 17, 47-50).

3. *On Church and State*. The precise relations between the two are discussed by neither writer. Where 2*H* is content to rebuke the Anabaptists for holding that Christians may not

serve in positions of civil authority (XXX 4), Calvin takes higher ground in expounding the God-given-ness of magisterial authority (asserted in 2*H* XXX 1; cf. *Inst.* IV 20, 1-7). On the question of war, 2*H* XXX 4 says that war is permissible 'only when all means to peace are exhausted'; nothing in Calvin corresponds to this. The 2*H* argument is that to uphold the rule of law a Christian may lay down his life (XXX 5); Calvin's is rather that the waging of war is part of the magistrate's duty as the upholder of law (IV 20, 11).

VI.—THE FRENCH AND BELGIC CONFESSIONS

THE French and Belgic Confessions are both faithfully Calvinistic documents, based on the teaching of the *Institutes*. The first National Synod of the Reformed Church of France was held in Paris in May 1559, moderated by François de Morel, Calvin's friend and pupil. The Confession which issued from that Synod is Calvin's own work. It is a relatively brief document (about 4,000 words), and was first written in the French tongue. It remained authoritative throughout the period (1559-1659) during which Synods of the French Reformed Church were held. Synods were suspended following the outlawing of the Protestant Church in France, until 1872, when the thirtieth Synod was held (that of 1659 having been the twenty-ninth). By that time the terms of the 1559 Confession were somewhat outdated, and a good deal of its authority had weakened and even died. The revived National Reformed Church, after much debate, accepted a very brief and moderate Confession, stating simply that the Church held the authority of the Scriptures, Justification by Faith in Jesus Christ, and the teaching expressed in the 'Apostles' Creed' and implied in the traditional liturgies of the Reformed Church. (See Schaff, *History of the Creeds of Christendom*, p. 500.)

The Belgic Confession, which closely follows that of Reformed France, was and remains authoritative for the Reformed Churches in Holland and Belgium, and (in translation) for the Dutch Reformed Church in America. It amplifies the French Confession, running to some 10,000 words, but substantially preserves its order and its doctrine. It was mainly written by Guido de Bres, a Dutch evangelist and martyr. It was first printed (probably) in 1562, and first accepted by the Synod of Antwerp, 1566; afterwards it was endorsed by Synods at Wesel (1568), Emden (1571), Dort (1574) and Middelburg (1581).

Finally it was declared authoritative, with certain modifications, at the Synod of Dort if 1619.

Since both Confessions follow so closely the teaching of Calvin, we need only here refer, and that briefly, to the manner in which they approach the special matters of Predestination, the Church and the Sacraments.

1. *Predestination.* F^1 VIII (under the general subject of Providence): 'We believe that God not only created all things, but that he governs and directs them, disposing and ordaining by his sovereign will all that happens in the world; not that he is the author of evil, or that the guilt of it can be imputed to him, as his will is the sovereign and infallible rule of all right and justice; but he hath wonderful means of so making use of devils and sinners that he can turn to good the evil which they do, and of which they are guilty. And thus, confessing that the providence of God orders all things, we humbly bow before the secrets which are hidden from us, without questioning what is above our understanding; but rather making use of what is revealed to us in Holy Scripture for our peace and safety, in as much as God, who has all things in subjection to himself, watches over us with a Father's care, so that not a hair of our heads shall fall without his will. And yet he restrains the devils and all our enemies, so that they cannot harm us without his leave.'

This is quoted in full because it comes from the same hand that wrote the *Institutes*. There could be no clearer proof that John Calvin, while in his theological treatise he pursued to its bitterest end the logic of Predestination, never felt that this doctrine should be incorporated in a Confession. And, of course it never has been so incorporated. There is in F one more passage on Predestination, in § XII: 'We believe that from this general corruption and condemnation in which all men are plunged, God, according to his eternal and immutable counsel, calleth those whom he hath chosen by his goodness and mercy alone in our Lord Jesus Christ, without consideration of their works, to display in them the riches of his mercy; leaving the

---

[1] French Confession: so from here on.

rest in the same corruption and condemnation to show in them his justice.' Election, then, was considered an article of Confession by Calvin, but not Predestination to perdition.

The Belgic Confession has in its Article XIII a declaration of Providence similar to that in *F* VIII, and its Article XVI, on 'Election', repeats briefly the teaching of *F*. Once again the iniquity of enquiring into God's mysteries is insisted on (XIII), and Election (XVI) is simply a statement of God's grace in calling some to share his beatitude.

2. *The Church*. (i) *F* XXV: The Church needs a ministry for its instruction, not because God stands in need of this, but because it has pleased him so to govern the Church. *B*[1] XXX. There must be a ministry to govern the Church who, forming a council of the Church with the Elders and Deacons, must guard the true doctrine. (XXXI) These Ministers, Elders and Deacons must be chosen by a lawful election of the Church, upon an attested calling. All Ministers have equal authority. (XXIII) They must not depart from the ordinances instituted by Christ.

(ii) *F* XXVI: Nobody should separate himself from the Church or forsake its assemblies, even though he be persecuted for doing so. *B* XXVIII says the same thing, adding that there is no salvation outside the Church.

(iii) *F* XXVII. The true Church is the company of the faithful who agree to follow the Word of God and the pure religion taught in it. Though among the faithful there may be hypocrites and reprobates, their iniquity cannot take away the right of the Church to be so called.

B XXIX. The marks of the true Church are: the right preaching of the Gospel, the administration of the Sacraments as instituted by Christ; the exercise of Church discipline. Faith is the mark of the believer. The false Church 'ascribes more power and authority to herself and her ordinances than to the Word of God'. The false Church does not administer the Sacraments as appointed by Christ but adds to them and takes from them as she thinks right. The false Church relies more

---

[1] Belgic Confession: so from here on.

on men than on Christ 'and persecutes those who live piously according to the Word of God and rebuke her for her errors'. Therefore the true and false Churches are easily to be distinguished.

(iv) *F* XXIX: There is no true Church where the Word of God is not received, nor profession made of subjection to it. Therefore we condemn the papal churches, where the sacraments are corrupted, falsified or destroyed. We hold that those who attend them are separated from the true Church. We admit, however, that some trace of the Church remains in the papal churches, and are able to admit the efficacy of papal *baptism*, not requiring rebaptism of those who leave the papal churches; but we cannot present our own children for its baptism.

(The emphasis in *B* is subtly different from that in *F*. *F* frankly repudiates Rome, while admitting that in it there is a vestige of the true Church. *B* distinguishes between the true and false Church, not naming but unmistakably describing the Roman churches. In *F* this does not look like a substitute for the doctrine of the Church visible and invisible; in *B* it almost does, though of course that is not what it is meant to be. But the doctrine of the visible and invisible Church is not mentioned in either *F* or *B*).

3. *The Sacraments.* (i) *F* XXXIV: The sacraments, ordained by God's grace for the strengthening of our weak faith, have their substance and truth in Jesus Christ, being in themselves 'only smoke and shadow'.

B XXXIII: The sacraments, being ordained (as above) . . . are 'visible signs and seals of an inward and invisible thing'. They are 'not vain or insignificant, so as to deceive us. For Jesus Christ is the true object presented by them, without whom they would be of no importance.'

(ii) *F* XXXV (beginning) = *B* XXXIII (end): There are two Sacraments only, as Christ instituted them.

(iii) *F* XXXV: *Baptism,* once received, lasts as long as life in its efficacy. The baptism of the children of believers is according to the mind of Christ.

B XXXIV: Baptism is the sacrament which Christ by the shedding of his blood substitutes for the human bloodshed of circumcision. It is a symbolic washing away of sin, and a sign of regeneration. Its efficacy depends not on the water but on the precious blood of Christ 'who is our Red Sea, through which we must pass to escape the tyranny of Pharaoh, that is, of the devil'. This baptism, once given, is efficacious for all life. Children of believers ought to receive it.

(iv) *F* XXXVI-XXXVIII: *The Lord's Supper* is a witness of the union which we have with Christ. Although he is in heaven, 'by the secret and incomprehensible power of his Spirit he feeds and strengthens us with the substance of his body and of his blood'. This is done 'spiritually'—this does not mean that we fancy or imagine it, but that it is a mystery that is beyond our reason and enquiry. All who come in faith receive that of which the Supper is a sign. God gives us really and effectually (*réellement et par effet*) what is set forth in the Sacrament. The bread and wine serve for our spiritual nourishment, and it is in this sense that the body of Jesus is our food and his blood our drink.

B XXXV: The regenerate live a twofold life—bodily and spiritual. Common bread nourishes the body, the living bread from heaven (Jesus Christ) nourishes the soul. The Sacrament of the Lord's Supper is instituted to represent to us (*figurer*) the spiritual bread. The manner of his working in us is beyond our understanding. He sits at the right hand of God but none the less makes us partakers of himself by faith. The fact that the Sacraments are conjoined with what they signify does not imply that all receive them in the same way: for unbelievers, not receiving the 'truth of the Sacrament', receive the elements of it to their condemnation.

(*Note:* Neither *B* nor *F* says any more than is here implied about Transubstantiation; *F* does not include the clause that is in *B* about the ungodly eating to their own damnation.)

4. *Magistrates. F* XXXIX-XL: The government of magistrates is God-given, and political discipline is conformable to the will of God. Citizens must be law-abiding, and obedience

to the secular authority of magistrates is the duty of the faithful.

B XXXVI, beginning as *F*, continues: 'God has given the magistrate the power of the sword . . . not only to watch over the welfare of the civil state, but also for the protection of the sacred ministry and the removal of idolatry and false worship.' Christians are required, as in *F*, to be subject to secular authority.

(*Note:* Nothing is said in either Confession about the right of the magistrate to wage war. It is only implied in his duty of preserving the public welfare and in the Christian's duty to obey him. *F*, though written by Calvin, does not contain the clause about the magistrate's duty to protect the ministry and put down idolatry. Protection of the church (in a less contentious form) is included in the magistrate's duties in *Inst.* IV 20, 3.)

The Synod of Dort, 1618-19

The Synod of Dort was the most impressive ecumenical gathering in Protestantism before the First Assembly of the World Council of Churches (1948). It met for six months, November 1618 to May 1619, and held 154 sessions. Of its 102 members, 58 were Dutchmen, the rest were representatives of the Reformed Churches of other countries. Its chief occasion was to discover the truth concerning the Arminian deviation from Calvinist Reformed doctrine, and the end of the Council was a complete victory for Calvinism.

Only one of the doctrines with which the present book is concerned was handled at length by the Council. It appears as the first of the five sections ('Heads of Doctrine') in the Canons of the Synod of Dort, published 1619, endorsed in France 1620 and 1623. Elsewhere than in France the Canons were given respect but not full authority. The Five Heads of Doctrine were Predestination, The Atonement, Man's Corruption, Conversion and the Perseverance of the Saints. (The third and fourth Heads were treated in one section.) Appended to the Canons were express repudiations of all heresies which disagreed with them. It is here only necessary to refer to the first Head, of *Predestination*, because while it repeats with due clarity and amplification what is declared in 2*H*, *F* and *B*, its statement concerning the Predestination of the reprobate to perdition is worth quoting as a classic and authoritative summary.

Article XV of the First Head of Doctrine runs thus (translated from the Latin as in the Constitutions of the Reformed Church in America): 'What peculiarly tends to illustrate and recommend to us the eternal and unmerited grace of election is the express testimony of sacred Scripture, that not all, but some only, are elected, while others are passed by in the eternal decree; whom God, out of his sovereign, most just, irreprehensible and unchangeable good pleasure, hath decreed to leave in the common misery into which they have wilfully plunged themselves, and not to bestow upon them saving faith and the grace of conversion; but permitting them in his just judgment to follow their own way; at last, for the declaration of his justice, to condemn and punish them for ever, not only on account of their unbelief, but also for all their other sins. And this is the decree of reprobation which by no means makes God the author of sin (the very thought of which is blasphemy), but declares him to be an awful, irreprehensible and righteous judge and avenger.'

Article XVI expressly states that this doctrine is not to be an occasion of anxiety for those who sincerely seek God and use the means of grace, though they have not yet found him: but that it is for the godly terror of those who openly disregard God and the salvation of Christ, and commit themselves to world worship.

Here we may conveniently summarize the doctrines of the Continental Confessions under the main heads we are discussing.

PREDESTINATION

A: Not mentioned.

FC: None is predestined to perdition. Predestination is to be predicated only of the elect (XI Aff. 4, 12; Neg. 3).

2H: Hope of election for all men may be entertained. It is wrong to say that predestination is for only a few. No teaching concerning predestination to perdition (X 4-6).

F: God has called those whom he has chosen, *leaving* the rest in the corruption of their sins (VIII).

B: Indistinguishable from *F* (XIII).

Institutes of John Calvin: Election is of those whom God has chosen. The others are positively predestined to perdition (III 21-3).

Dort adopts the form of words incorporated in *F* and *B*, including the verb *'leave'*; but teaches explicitly that not all are, or can be hoped to be, called (thus contradicting *2H*).

THE CHURCH

A: The Church is the congregation of saints where the Word is rightly preached and the Sacraments rightly administered. Its unity depends on this, and not on uniformity of ceremonies.

FC: Nothing is added to the teaching of *A*.

2H:

(1) There is one universal Church: the Church militant and the Church Triumphant are in communion with one another.

(2) The Church does not err so long as it is founded in the teaching of Apostles and Prophets.

(3) Christ being the Church's immediate head needs no Vicar.

(4) Outside Christ there is no salvation.

(5) The Church is invisible (i.e. its membership is known only to God).

(6) Unity lies not in ceremonies but in obedience to the Apostolic Faith. (XVII.)

F: The Church is the company of the Faithful, which may contain reprobates. Nobody should separate himself from the Church.

B: The marks of the Church are the right preaching of the Gospel, the administration of the (two) Sacraments, and the exercise of discipline. True Church distinguished from false in giving itself more authority than the Word of God.

All the Calvinistic Confessions follow closely, though all select from rather than repeating comprehensively, the teaching of Calvin in *Inst.* IV 1-19.

THE SACRAMENTS

A: The Sacraments are signs of God's goodwill towards us. They must be so administered that faith has free course. The doctrine of *ex opere operato* is repudiated (XIII).

FC: See next section on the Lord's Supper. Nothing added to the general teaching of *A* on the Sacraments.

2H:

(1) Two sacraments, not seven.
(2) Sacraments of the New Israel fulfil the promises set forth by those (circumcision and Paschal Lamb) of the Old.
(3) Sacraments contain the word, the sign, and the thing signified.
(4) The signs are not changed into the things signified. (XIX.)

F: The sacraments, ordained by God for the believer's comfort, have their substance in Christ. There are two only.

B: Repeats the argument of *F*.

All the Calvinistic Confessions follow closely the teaching of Calvin in *Inst.* IV 14-16.

BAPTISM

A: Baptism is necessary to salvation. Children who die unbaptized cannot inherit salvation (IX).

FC: nothing added to the teaching of *A*.

2H:

(1) Baptism is of Christ's institution.
(2) One baptism is effective for life.
(3) Baptism is a washing away of sin and a refreshment of the soul.

(4) We are baptized into one body of the Church.
(5) Emergency baptism prohibited because women are
    not permitted to administer office in the Church
    (XX).

F: Baptism is of lifelong efficacy (XXXV).

B: Baptism symbolically washes away sin and is a sign of
regeneration. It is of lifelong efficacy. Its efficacy depends not
on the water but on the blood of Christ (XXXVI).

All the Confessions agree in permitting infant baptism and
anathematizing the Anabaptist opposition to it.

THE LORD'S SUPPER

A:

(1) The body and blood of Christ are truly present (X).
(2) Private masses, masses celebrated for money, masses
    multiplied and masses said in foreign tongues are
    denounced (*De Ab*. III). But the Mass itself is not
    abolished.

FC: Christ is truly and substantially present in the Bread
and Wine. The Body and Blood are taken with the mouth, not
merely spiritually; but not literally taken with the mouth, but
'in a heavenly and supernatural manner'. Transubstantiation
is rejected, because the true doctrine teaches that there is no
change in the substance of the elements. Not the words of
institution but the faith of the believer work the change from
the natural to the supernatural mode of eating. Unbelievers
eat to their condemnation (VII).

2H: The Supper is a constant renewal of Remembrance. It
is partaken by *manducatio spiritualis* and *manducatio sacramentalis* (XX).

F: Christ, being in heaven, yet feeds us mysteriously and is
present with us. We partake 'really and spiritually' (XXVI-
XXVIII).

B: The Sacrament represents spiritual nourishment. The
sign is conjoined with the thing signified: but not for
unbelievers.

Opposition to Transubstantiation is always implied but not always explicit in the Calvinist Confessions.

CHURCH AND STATE

All the Confessions agree that magistracy is ordained of God, and that Christians need not have scruples about taking civil office.

The duty of the magistrate to protect the welfare of the state is mentioned in all the Confessions. His duty to protect the ministry and the Church is explicit in *B* and in *Inst.* IV 20, 3.

The pacifist beliefs of the Anabaptists are always denied by implication, but the duty of the Christian to bear arms at the call of the magistrate is explicit only in *A* XVI, *2H* XXX and *Inst.*

VII.—THE THIRTY-NINE ARTICLES OF THE CHURCH OF ENGLAND

The Ten Articles of 1536

In the words of John Foxe the martyrologist, this first Confession of the new-born Anglican Church was designed for 'weaklings newly weaned from their mother's milk of Rome'. They were designed by King Henry VIII himself to ensure that, apart from the necessity (as he saw it) of repudiating the authority of the Pope of Rome, the Catholic Faith should be held unimpaired in England; and its Preface (written by the King) declares the royal intention of repressing and extinguishing all dissent against that doctrine. Therefore the Confession is made under the following ten heads:

1. The binding authority of Scripture, the three Ecumenical Creeds, and the first four Ecumenical Councils (Nicaea, A.D. 325, Constantinople 381, Ephesus 431, Chalcedon 451).

2. The necessity of baptism for salvation and the certainty that unbaptized infants will not be saved.

3. The sacraments of penance, with confession and absolution, are both expedient and necessary.

4. In the Eucharist the body and blood of Christ are 'substantially, really and corporally present' in the bread and wine.

5. Justification by faith is taught, joined with charity and obedience.

6. Images are permitted in churches.

7. The saints and the Virgin Mary are to be honoured in worship.

8. The saints may be invoked in prayer.

9. Certain rites and ceremonies are prescribed, such as the giving of ashes on Ash Wednesday, the procession of candles at Candlemas, the sprinkling of holy water and the use of clerical vestments.

10. The doctrine of purgatory is affirmed and prayers for the dead in purgatory are permitted.

This then is a restatement of traditional Roman doctrine, simply omitting any reference to the nature of the Church and the authority of the Pope.

The Bishops' Book (1537) and The King's Book (1543)

The Ten Articles were a minimal statement. They were too brief either to form a complete Confession or to provide that explication and commentary which the sixteenth century demanded. The Church of England never committed itself to treatises of an official sort as lengthy and comprehensive as the Second Helvetic Confession or the Formula of Concord or the Second Part of the Augsburg Confession. In their final form the Thirty-nine Articles are singularly precise and laconic: but by way of comment and explanation two early books were published, *The Bishops' Book* of 1537 and *The King's Book* of 1543. *The Bishops' Book*, largely influenced by Cranmer and Ridley, contains expositions of the Creed, the Ten Commandments, the Lord's Prayer and the Ave Maria, followed by a discussion of Justification and of Purgatory. The title of the book as first published was *The Institution of a Christian Man*. The King accepted the draft of it, signed by the two archbishops, the nineteen bishops, and twenty-five other theologians, and directed that portions of it be read in churches throughout the country every Sunday for three years.

But the royal approval, when the King began to study the book closely, was modified by doubts concerning even that very tentative approach to Reformed doctrine which marked in it an advance on the Ten Articles. A commission was set up in 1540, consisting of eight bishops and twelve theologians, to deliberate things 'which pertain to the institution of a Christian man'. The result of these deliberations, in the course of which the doctrines of the Church were closely examined and subjected to the stress of keen debate,[1] was *A Necessary Doctrine and Erudition for any Christian Man commonly known as The King's Book* (1543). It kept much of the language of the earlier book, but (*a*) produced a new article on the meaning of Faith, (*b*) rewrote the articles on Baptism and the Sacraments, and (*c*) substituted for the note on Justification three articles on Free Will, Justification and Good Works.

This acute analysis (which the Council of Trent in its Sixth Session could perhaps have used with advantage) leads to the statement that when we say we are justified by faith, we mean not faith as distinguished from hope and charity, but faith including hope and charity. It is further argued that a man may offend God without losing his *faith*; for a man can commit an offence which separates him from faith (in the second, inclusive sense), but still be not separated from faith (in the first, exclusive sense) which looks for God's forgiveness.

The section ends by saying that although God's promises in Christ are immutable, human promises are not: and therefore we must not claim assurance of salvation such as would make us overlook the consequences of our own defections. Faith (first sense) is the condition of those who hope for triumph but who have not triumphed yet.

Of *Baptism*, *The King's Book* says that Baptism removes the guilt of original sin from whoever is baptized, child or grown-up, and that there remains only the tendency to concupiscence

---

[1] On Faith, *The King's Book* distinguishes two meanings:

(*a*) 'A several gift of God by itself, distinct from hope and charity; so taken, it signifieth a persuasion and belief wrought by God in man's heart, whereby he assenteth, granteth, and taketh for true, not only that God is . . . but also that all the words and sayings of God which be revealed and opened in the scripture, be of most certain truth and infallible verity.'

(*b*) 'Faith in the second acception is considered as it hath hope and charity annexed and joined unto it: and faith so taken, signifieth not only the belief and persuasion before mentioned in the first acception, but also a sure confidence and hope to attain whatsoever God hath promised for Christ's sake, and an hearty love to God, and obedience to his commandments.'

in the person baptized (that is, to self-will and self-pleasing). Of the necessity of Baptism, it says, 'Seeing that out of the Church neither infants nor no man else can be saved, they must needs be christened and cleansed by baptism, and so incorporated into the Church.' Baptism can never be received more than once. (There is no positive comment on the fate of unbaptized children.)

Of the *Lord's Supper*, the Book endorses the doctrine that the body and blood of Christ are wholly present in the Sacrament, but with an unusual emphasis which also endorses the Roman doctrine of communion in one kind. The whole of Christ is comprehended in the bread; and, as a living body cannot be without blood, so we may suppose equally that the Blood of Christ is comprehended also in the bread. Therefore communion in two kinds is unnecessary for the faithful.[1] But the whole emphasis of this long and moving chapter is on the state of faith in the believer, which is more important than any directions about the manner in which the Sacrament is delivered to him, and the necessity of his approaching it in reverence and after due preparation. It is a doctrinal *tour de force*, in harmonizing as it does the Roman practice of communion in one kind with the Lutheran teaching of the primacy of faith, and a respect for traditional ceremony with a concession to the moral and intellectual demands of the new age.

On *Free Will*, the Book distinguishes between the condition of man before and after the Fall. Before the Fall man had power to obey or to disobey; after it, the faculties are so darkened that free will is incapable of performing 'spiritual and heavenly things', however much power it may still have to take decisions relevant merely to earthly life. This agrees with *A* XVIII; *2H* IX takes the argument into a third category of the freedom of the Justified.

On *Justification*, the Book distinguishes between the 'first Justification', by which we 'first come into God's house', being graciously deemed by God to have a righteousness which of ourselves we could not claim, and 'increase of Justification',

[1] *The King's Book*, ed. T. A. Lacey (1932), pp. 53-4.

concerning which it roundly dismisses all devaluation of perseverance and good works. All the gifts and graces of God contribute to our 'waxing and increasing in justification', and we must diligently, and in remembrance of our own 'pronity to sin', cultivate these virtues and not assent to the temptations of the devil. Therefore we are justified 'by faith' only in as much as 'faith' is taken in the 'second acception' above, not 'by faith' considered as a single virtue pre-eminent above the rest. We cannot be justified without the performance of good works of perseverance: but we may not ascribe our justification to these good works. It is given freely and not for any merit of ours. The implications of this are discussed further in the concluding section on Good Works.

This able and astute treatise proved, however, too reactionary for the mounting force of Reformed opinion in England, and it will be found that in many respects the Thirty-nine Articles are more radical.

The presence of radical opinions is well attested by the necessity of passing the Act of Six Articles (1539), which is chiefly directed against Anabaptist and Lollard opinions. These articles, incorporated in the Act (31 Henry VIII cap. 14), declare (1) that the natural body and blood of Christ are really present under the form of the bread and wine in the Eucharist; and after the consecration there remains no substance of bread or wine, nor any substance but that of Christ; (2) that communion in both kinds is not necessary for salvation; (3) that priests may not marry; (4) that vows of chastity or widowhood must be kept and respected; (5) that private masses be continued in the English Church, and (6) that auricular confession is to be continued. The Act prescribed death by burning and confiscation of property for breach of the first article, and for the others, confiscation for the first offence and death for the second.

Reformation of doctrine was, however, the keynote of the *Forty-Two Edwardine Articles* of 1553 and the *Thirty-Nine Elizabethan Articles* (1563, Latin version: 1571, authorized English Translation).

The Edwardine Articles

The Edwardine Articles were probably never authorized by Convocation, but only circulated fairly widely among the clergy. They differ from the Thirty-nine in only the following respects:

(1) An article included in 1553 and excluded in 1563 on the sin against the Holy Ghost (XVI).

(2) An article on the resurrection of the dead (XXXIX).

(3) An article against antinomianism (XIX).

(4) An article on the condition of the soul after death, in answer to the Anabaptist doctrine of 'psychopannuchia' (XL).

(5) An article against the millennarians (XLI).

(6) An article denying universal salvation (XLII).

(7) The inclusion on Article III (1563) of a clause on the Descent of Christ into Hades, omitted in 1563.

(8) A protest in Article XXIX against the ubiquitarian doctrine, omitted in 1563.

The period 1553-8, during which Queen Mary reigned in England, saw the suppression of all open Protestant activity. In consequence the Forty-two Articles lay in abeyance. In 1559 Archbishop Matthew Parker revised them into a series of Eleven Articles, avoiding controversial topics and differing wholly in their arrangement. In 1563 these were incorporated into the Thirty-nine Articles, which have remained since that date authoritative, though they are interpreted with great latitude, throughout the Anglican Communion (with minor adjustments for American Episcopal Churches, incorporated in the American revision of 1801).

The Thirty-Nine Articles

The Thirty-nine Articles in their English edition of 1571 are reprinted in full in any edition of the English Book of Common Prayer. Here therefore comment alone is necessary, and that only on the controverted points.

The Articles are, like the Church of England itself, a meeting-place of Catholic and Protestant doctrine which is quite unique in the records of Christian Confessions. They show intimate knowledge not only of Roman doctrine but of the Augsburg Confession and the Calvinist statements. They incorporate doctrines of both the Lutheran and the Reformed versions of the Faith. Echoes of the thought and (in the Latin original) even of the actual words of the Augsburg Confession are to be found in Articles I, II, IV, V and IX, and of the Wurtemburg Confession (1552: a modification of *A* which never became widely authoritative) in II, V, VI, X, XI, XII and XX. In particular we may note the Lutheran influence in such phrases as these:

XI (*Justification*): 'We are accounted righteous before God, only for the merit of our Lord and Saviour Jesus Christ, by faith and not for our own works or deservings.' (Cf. *A* IV, *W* 5.)

XIX (*The Church*): 'The [visible] Church of Christ is a congregation of faithful men, in the which the pure Word of God is preached, and the Sacraments be duly administered.' (Cf. *A* VII.)

XXV (*The Sacraments*): 'Sacraments ordained of Christ be not only badges or tokens of Christian men's profession, but rather they be certain sure witnesses, and effectual signs of grace, and God's good will towards us, by the which he doth work invisibly in us.' (Cf. *A* XIII.)

In the doctrinal Articles I and II there are similar reminiscences and even quotations from *A* I and III.

On the other hand, the contacts which the Marian exiles had personally with the Continental Reformers of the French and Swiss schools ensured that some of the Calvinist notes would sound prominently in the Articles as they were finally published. In particular, Henry Bullinger, of Zürich, is attested by letters written to him from Bishop Horn of Winchester and

Grinal in London in 1563 and 1575 to have been a notable
apologist for Calvinism to the Englishmen who were seeking a
Reformed Confession.

The most remarkable gesture towards Calvinism in the
Articles is XVII, which deals with Predestination. Among
other propositions, it states that there is a predestination of
men to everlasting life, that the predestinate cannot perish,
that not all men are predestinate, but that those who are are
called outwardly by the Word and inwardly by the Spirit of
God; the predestinate are justified by faith, sanctified by the
Holy Spirit, and will be glorified in the eternal world. Predestination is a doctrine of comfort to the godly, of terror only
to the carnal-minded.[1]

One must bear in mind the date—1559-1563: the Calvinist
Confessions were still in the making. The Second Helvetic was
not published until 1566. Article XVII thus stands as one of
the first authoritative confessional statements on Predestination, and it can easily be seen to embody the Calvinist teaching
(that is, the teaching of Calvin's Instruction in Faith, and of
the Confessions which subsequently emerged, though not of
Inst. III) as it would have been communicated by Bullinger
and his colleagues. There is no word of predestination to
perdition; but on the other hand there is no hint either that
all men are, or may be hoped to be, predestined to glory (which
is more than hinted at in 2H X). The insistence on God's
sovereignty and on the terror with which this sovereignty is
to be regarded by the disobedient is strictly Calvinistic. It
will be remembered that A does not refer to Predestination,
and that FC applied it only to the elect. The Articles
simply state God's sovereignty, and imply that he *could*,
but not necessarily that he does, predestine men to disobedience, laying all the emphasis on the glory laid up for
the obedient.

---

[1] These are six of the ten propositions drawn from Article XVII by
Thomas Rogers (d. 1616), chaplain to Archbishop Bancroft, in the
first commentary to be written in English on the Articles. (See Schaff,
History of the Creeds of Christendom, p. 636, and comments there.)

H

Baptism. Article XXVII declares that Baptism is not only a 'sign of profession and mark of difference' distinguishing Christians from the unchristened, but also 'a sign of Regeneration of New-Birth, whereby, as by an instrument, they that receive Baptism rightly are grafted into the Church; the promises of the forgiveness of sins and our adoption to be the sons of God by the Holy Ghost are visibly signed and sealed; Faith is confirmed, and Grace increased by virtue of prayer unto God'. Here is positive doctrine only; nothing is stated about the necessity of baptism for salvation. The 1549 Prayer Book, however, includes this phrase in the opening prayer at Public Baptism: 'that they, being delivered from thy wrath, may be received into the ark of Christ's Church, and so saved from perishing'. This acknowledgment of the necessity of baptism for salvation was excised in the 1552 Book, where the corresponding phrase reads: 'that they, being delivered from thy wrath, may be received into the ark of Christ's Church, and being stedfast in faith, joyful through hope, and rooted in charity, may so pass the ways of this troublesome world, that finally they may come to the land of everlasting life.' This was retained in 1662 and represents a movement from the conservative Lutheran view (*A* IX) to the Calvinist position. The close connexion between baptism and regeneration is, of course, both Calvinist and Catholic.

Article XVI declares that not all sin after Baptism is unpardonable (thus denouncing the Anabaptist position), and denies also that it is impossible to sin after baptism. This also is consistent both with the Calvinist position and with the findings of the Council of Trent.

On *The Sacraments* generally, Article XXV takes again a Reformed position in declaring that there are two, not seven (the five rejected having partly 'grown up of the corrupt following of the Apostles') and being partly 'states of life allowed in the Scriptures'. The findings of Trent are contradicted in the clause which forbids the 'carrying about' and 'gazing upon' of the Sacraments, and the general doctrine that the Sacraments are 'not only badges or tokens of Christian men's profession, but rather certain sure witnesses and effectual signs of grace and God's good will towards us' comes, as we have already seen, from Augsburg and is also conformable with Calvinism and with Catholic teaching.

On the *Lord's Supper*, Articles XXVIII-XXXI steer a middle course through the hazards of Reformed doctrine. Transubstantiation is declared unscriptural in XXVIII, and it is stated that 'the Body of Christ is given, taken and eaten only after an heavenly and spiritual manner. The means by which the Body of Christ is received and eaten in the Supper is Faith.'

This could hardly be further both from Tridentine doctrine and from that of *A* and *FC*, both of which last are concerned to preserve as much as can be preserved of Catholic doctrine at this point. It cuts through the technicalities which were subsequently written into 2*H*, and even the cautious statement of *F* (1559) is bolder than what is here written.

Article XXIX proved on its publication to be controversial. It states, in conformity with Calvinist teaching, that 'the Wicked, and such as be void of a lively faith, although they do carnally and visibly press with their teeth . . . the Sacrament of the Body and Blood of Christ, yet in no wise are they partakers of Christ, but rather to their condemnation do eat and drink the sign or Sacrament of so great a thing'. This article, which appears in the manuscript of 1563, was omitted in all printed copies until the definitive edition of 1571, probably because Queen Elizabeth herself was displeased with it. But it was then restored, and of course its teaching is again Calvinist. The Catechism on this point reinforces the teaching by saying that the benefits of the Supper are received 'by the faithful'.

Article XXX simply states that communion in both kinds is to be the rule of the Church. Article XXXI insists that the Mass is not a sacrifice. Since Christ made his Sacrifice once for all, to say that the Priest offers Christ as a sacrifice in the Mass is 'blasphemous fable and dangerous deceit'. This directly contradicts the findings of Trent (Session XXII, Decree § 1), and reinforces the teaching of Luther in the *Babylonish Captivity*.[1]

In these concerns, then, the Articles will be seen to be largely influenced by the movements of Reformation thought. There can be no doubt of the importance to their final form of the Marian exile, which threw so many English Protestants into the company of the Swiss and French Reformers just at the time when Calvinist doctrine was finally forming itself. This episode more than anything else must have caused the authors of the Articles to break away from the conservatism of Henry VIII's Ten Articles and later Six Articles. Article XXXII of the Thirty-nine, for example, directly contradicts the third of the Six Articles (1539) in permitting the marriage of priests, and the doctrine of the large sections we have just discussed shows a clean break with that Roman tradition which Henry VIII was anxious to see preserved under his own headship.

At the same time, the diplomatic tone of the Thirty-nine Articles is something unique in the literature of the classic Confessions; this is witnessed by the astonishing variety of interpretations which later ages have been able to put on many of the Articles, and the diversity of uses within the later Church of England (and indeed within that of the present day) which can be felt not to constitute contradiction of what is there written. The judgment of Philip Schaff, made in 1877, still has point: 'Moderate High-Churchmen and Arminians, who dislike Calvinism, represent them as purely Lutheran; Anglo-Catholics and Tractarians, who abhor both Lutheranism and Calvinism, endeavour to conform them as much as possible to the contemporary decrees of the Council of Trent; Calvinistic and evangelical Low-Churchmen find in them substantially their own creed.'[2] It is the distinguishing quality of this document that alone of the sixteenth-century Confessions it seeks to accommodate diverse views rather than to separate its own from those of other bodies.

This may well have something to do with the fact that in

---

[1] Lee-Woolf, *op. cit.*, pp. 250 ff.
[2] Schaff, *History of the Creeds of Christendom*, p. 622.

subsequent controversies between Christian bodies of opinion in Britain it was on the whole not those massive concerns of Predestination and the Lord's Supper and Baptism on which the disputes centred, but rather on the doctrine of the Church. There are notable exceptions, of course. The Baptists were naturally intolerant of the teaching in the Articles about Baptism; and of course, just as it was possible to assimilate the teaching of the Articles to any one of several distinct schools of thought, so it was equally possible for any who followed one of those schools to find much that was objectionable in those parts of the Articles which reflected the thought of the others. In Britain it was the Calvinists who objected most strongly to what they deemed to be concessions to Rome. English puritanism was born of an objection to doctrinal compromise. (It may be no more than an historical coincidence, but the first recorded use of the word 'puritan' for decided Calvinistic opinion in England is dated in the year following the publication of the Latin version of the Articles.)

The Church is treated in Articles XIX, XX, XXI, and matters of discipline in XXIII, XXIV, XXXVIII; kindred matters are treated in XXXV-XXXIX.

Article XIX declares that 'the visible Church of Christ is a congregation of faithful men, in the which the pure Word of God is preached, and the Sacraments be duly ministered according to Christ's ordinance, in all those things that of necessity are requisite to the same'. Here is language closely parallel to that of *A*, but the word 'visible' is a Calvinistic word. Nothing is said in the Articles about the Church Invisible. The Sacraments are, be it noted, to be administered with such rites as are *necessary*. In the second paragraph the Church of Rome is said to have erred both in matters of Ceremony and in matters of Faith.

Article XX says that the Church has power to decree rites and ceremonies, and authority in matters of faith; but that although the Church is 'keeper of Holy Writ', it must enact nothing that is contrary to it, or even that is in conformity with one part but in contradiction of another part.

Article XXI says that General Councils may not be called 'without the commandment and will of princes', and that when they are gathered their authority cannot be held binding except it be shown to be derived from Scripture.

Article XXIII says that none may minister in the Church who are not lawfully called 'by men who have public authority in the Congregation' to call them. Article XXIV says that everything spoken in church must be in a language that the people understand. Article XXXVIII, which denies that Christians hold all goods in common, is directed against a primitive Anabaptist belief, held by the followers of Hutter, that Christians should have all things in common.

Article XXXIII, of *Excommunication*, teaches that any person excommunicated by the Church must be avoided by all Christians until he be 'openly reconciled by penance'.

Article XXXIV, of the *Traditions of the Church*, explains that Ceremonies need not be uniform in all places, and that they may be, in so far as they are man-made, changed anywhere and at any time; but that where they are manifestly scriptural, alteration of them is to be deemed an offence 'against the common order of the Church, against the authority of the Magistrate, and against the consciences of the weak brethren'.

Article XXXV prescribes the homilies that are to be read in Church. Article XXXVI, of the *Consecration of Bishops and Ministers*, enacts that only those who are consecrated and ordained according to the Prayer Book 'of Edward the sixth' (that is, of 1552) are lawfully consecrated and ordained.

Article XXXVII, of *Church and State*, lays down that the sovereign is the supreme governor of the Church. It is carefully explained that this does not give authority to the sovereign to minister in word and sacraments, but that it merely acknowledges the rule of the sovereign over all her subjects. It says further than the bishop of Rome has no authority in England, that Christians are not exempt from the death penalty, and that they may at the bidding of the secular power serve in war.

Article XXXIX explains that a Christian, though profane

and frivolous swearing is forbidden, may swear an oath at the bidding of the magistrate.

While certain of these articles are self-explanatory either in themselves or by context (namely, XX, XXI, XXIV, XXXIII, XXXIV, XXXV, XXXVIII and XXXIX), the others will bear brief commentary.

At certain points the Articles show a leaning towards a Calvinist doctrine of the Church: for example, where the word 'visible' is used (XIX), and where the Magistrate's power and obligation to defend and rule the country is implied (XXXVII). But on the whole the doctrine of the Church here enshrined is peculiar to the Church of England, both in its evasiveness and in certain particulars.

It is clear, for example, that without the other half of the Calvinist statement (concerning the Church invisible), Article XIX is so vague as to include any doctrine whatever, since all depends on what is a congregation of faithful men and what, in the administration of Word and Sacrament, is deemed right. We are able to infer certain other doctrines which are implicit elsewhere in the Articles, such as the authority of the Prayer Book (XXXVI) and the necessity of the lawful ordination of the Ministry. But from Article XXXVI we can gather nothing concerning the Apostolic Succession, which is not mentioned in the Articles, and indeed there is not a word from end to end of the section on the Church (XIX-XXXIX) which suggests any specifically Catholic doctrine. The Catholicity of the Articles resides only in their acceptance of the three Creeds, the Trinitarian Faith, and the sufficiency of the Scriptures for Salvation (I-VIII). Here it is only in the separation of the books of the Old Testament Apocrypha as being for 'instruction' but not for 'the establishment of doctrine' that any significant exception is taken to Catholic doctrine.

But except in its implied acceptance of the phrase 'One holy Catholic and Apostolic Church' in the 'Nicene Creed', there is no overt catholicity in the doctrine of the Church that the Articles expound. True, it may be held to be implicit in Article XIX, but no more than that.

On the other hand, the intention of Article XXXVII (whatever may have been the intention of Henry VIII when he inaugurated the doctrine of the sovereign's sole headship of the English Church) is very far from what its enemies took it to be. With an astuteness which is never absent from their devices, the authors of the Articles softened Henry's hard doctrine, which was hateful alike to Catholics and Evangelicals, by allying a statement about the sovereign's sole governorship with an implied denunciation of one form of antinomianism. There were enthusiasts who believed that membership of the true Church absolved them from their obligations toward their rulers. The manner in which XXXVII is expressed makes it clear that this doctrine, at any rate, is not to be tolerated. What later ages made of XXXVII is quite another matter. There is nothing in the Article as stated that obliges the Church to consult the sovereign before appointing its bishops, or to consult Parliament before modifying its Prayer Book. That all belongs to the British Constitution, which is no concern of ours here. It is not stated in the Articles.

One other thing must be said. The Articles are designed to be the Rule of Faith, not of what we now think of as the 'Church of England' (one Christian group among others), but of every English Christian. Therefore set around them were regulations concerning church attendance, subscription to the Articles, and general conformity in religion which are in no way explicit in the Articles themselves, but which became the chief point at which the whole system for which the Articles stood was attacked by Dissenters. No document of the kind is more difficult to see purely theologically and without an historical bias than the Thirty-nine Articles. For example: it is always difficult to read Article XXXVI concerning the authority of the Prayer Book without having in mind the ejection of Dissenting ministers in 1662 for non-conformity to it; or what is said in XXXVII about the sovereign's Supreme Headship without seeing the figure of Whitgift and the Tyburn Executions in the background. Moreover, the Articles are not primarily a document of Dissent in the sense that all the other documents so far considered in this book except the minutes of the Council of Trent are documents of Dissent. The legal sanctions against dissent from the Articles were more formidable than those against Dissent from the regulations of Calvin's Church in Geneva. The Articles dissented from Trent, but much more were designed to be part of an English Establishment. But all this is foreign to a discussion of their actual contents. It is merely a caution against judging their contents in the light of contemporary history and politics. Within the Articles is a theology which is more enduring than the passing phases of history or politics.

VIII.—OTHER ENGLISH-SPEAKING
CONFESSIONS, 1560-1658

THE SCOTTISH CONFESSION OF FAITH, 1560

In the year 1560 was held the first General Assembly of the Church of Scotland, and the first Confession of that Church was published. The Church of Scotland was formally recognized and established by the Scottish Parliament in 1567, but the foundation of the Church of Scotland could be dated ten years before that establishment, in as much as in December 1557 a body of Protestant nobles and gentlemen signed in Edinburgh a Covenant 'to maintain, nourish and defend to the death the whole Congregation of Christ and every member thereof' (Congregation meaning, here as in the Thirty-nine Articles, Church).

The first and authentic edition of the 1560 Confession was written in contemporary Scottish, very largely by John Knox himself. It reads less like a series of Articles than most Confessions, and more like a connected theological treatise. Its length is moderate—some 8,000 words. It differs very little from the Calvinist statements that emerged on the Continent, but its tone is more measured than theirs usually is, and its text is free from close theological argument concerning technicalities.

The Doctrines of God (I), Creation (II), Original Sin (III), Revelation (IV), the Incarnation (VI-VII), the Passion, Resurrection and Ascension of Christ (IX-XI), the Holy Spirit (XII) and of the Authority of Scripture (XIX) are set forth in a manner that calls for no comment here. Other matters are handled as we are about to show.

Election (VIII). The paragraph on Election comes between those on the Incarnation and that on the Passion, and is concerned with election and predestination only in so far as they are associated with texts in St. John's Gospel (i. 13 and xx. 17). Election equals 'being given power to become the sons of God'. No more is said about it than this.

The Church (V, XVI). Here the approach is unusual, in that an early paragraph (V) teaches of 'The Continuance, Increase and Preservation of the Kirk' between the paragraphs on Revelation and on the Incarnation. This paragraph is designed to show how the Old Israel is preserved in faith to prepare the way for the new Israel. This is a doctrine which receives prominence in all Calvinist teaching, but Knox's insertion of it here, instead of alongside the paragraph on 'The Kirk', is unusual.

This teaching is taken up in § XVI, which opens by saying that there always has been, and will be to the end of the world, a Church. It is Catholic (explained as meaning 'universal') 'because it contains the elect of all ages, realms, nations and tongues'. It is therefore called the Communion of Saints. Outside the Church there is no life 'nor eternal felicity'. The Church is invisible, known only to God, and includes those who yet live and those who have died in faith.

The departed elect are called (§ XVII) the 'church militant' (an unusual use of that phrase). The True Kirk is distinguished (§ XVIII) from the 'filthy synagogue' (alternatively styled 'that horrible harlot the Kirk malignant') by clear and true notes, namely, the preaching of the Word, the right administration of the Sacraments, and the proper ministry of Church discipline. Wherever these notes are seen, there is the true Church of Christ.

By The Word is meant the Scriptures of the Old and New Testament, whose interpreter is neither any private nor public person, however eminent, nor any single Church, however distinguished, but the Holy Spirit, 'by which also the Scripture was written'. Anything said by any 'doctor, Kirk or Council' which is repugnant to the doctrine of Scripture must be disregarded. Further (§ XIX) is it error to suppose that the authority of Scripture must be received through the Church; the Church must be obedient to Scripture.

The doctrine about General Councils (XX) is the same as that in the Thirty-nine Articles.

No form of Church government is laid down in this treatise, apart from what must be assumed to be conformable with § XIX and the teaching that all ministers are of equal authority before the Word of God. The logical consequence of this is, of course, Presbyterianism.

The Sacraments (XXI-XXIII). Both Sacraments are treated together in the three paragraphs 'Of the Sacraments', 'Of the Right Administration of the Sacraments' and 'To whom Sacraments appertain'. The doctrine here is not widely different from that of the Thirty-nine Articles, but it is more amply expressed, and sounds more of the authentic Calvinist notes. For example, in § XXI the opening statement concerns the alliance between the sacraments of the Old Testament and those of the New, and goes on at once to assert that the Church's Sacraments effect 'a most blessed conjunction, union and society' of the elect with their Head, Christ Jesus. To say that Sacraments are 'nothing else but naked and bare signs' is 'vanity' and utterly condemned. It is rather to be held that 'by Baptism we are ingrafted in Christ Jesus to be made partakers of his justice, by the which our sins are covered and remitted; and also that in the supper, rightly used, Christ Jesus is so joined with us, that He becomes the very nourishment and food of our souls'. Transubstantiation is 'pernicious doctrine' and a 'damnable belief'; we believe rather in a union effected by the Holy Spirit, who 'makes us feed upon the body and blood of Christ Jesus, which was once broken and shed for us, which is now in heaven'. The doctrine of the Ascension is then closely associated with the Supper. Worship is not to be offered to the 'signs' (that is, the Elements), but only to Christ. The signs are to be used with reverence and faith.

For the right administration of the Sacraments (XXII) there must be a lawful ministry to dispense them, and the proper elements to be dispensed. Priests of the Church of Rome are 'no ministers of Christ Jesus'. Women may not baptize. The cup is not to be withheld from the people, and the Sacrament

is not to be displayed or carried about. Any conduct (such as
abounds in the Mass) which suggests that the priest is a mediator between God and man, or that the operation is a sacrifice
in itself, is abhorrent.

The Sacraments are for the use of the faithful and their
children (XXIII). Therefore children are to be baptized,
despite their defective understanding. The Supper is to be
offered only to those 'who are of the household of faith'.
Partaking without faith, or in an uncharitable state of mind, is
forbidden.

Church and State. The secular power is a gift of God and to
be respected by all Christians. Furthermore, it is given to
'kings, princes, rulers and magistrates' to reform and purge
religion, to maintain its truth, to suppress idolatry and
superstition. (A very close alliance between the Reformed
Church and the civil power is here presupposed, as it was in
Geneva. A capacity in secular rulers for purging religion was
assumed which later ages have not dared to assume. The origin
of this was the conception of priesthood within kingship which
prevails in the Old Testament, and the alliance between the
two forms of power in the medieval Church which was taken
over uncriticized in the political movements of the Continental
Reformation. The Thirty-nine Articles by-passed this doctrine
with their teaching in Article XXXVII that the sovereign is
supreme governor of the Church. Certain English Dissenters,
notably the Brownists, opposed unambiguously any notion of
the Church's alliance with secular power.)

THE WESTMINSTER CONFESSION, 1647

The Westminster Confession was published at the end of the
doctrinal sessions of the Westminster Assembly of Divines
(1643-7: the Assembly continued in a desultory fashion into
the year 1648), to provide a rule of faith for that Presbyterian
Church which it hoped to see as the one Church of England.
Dissent against the Church of England after the Elizabethan
Settlement of 1571 had taken many forms: Presbyterian,

Congregational and Baptist principally. After the executions of the Brownists (the earliest advocates of the Independent or Congregational Way, see below, p. 122) in 1593 men of the Independent view of churchmanship (who from about 1600 included those who dogmatically opposed infant baptism) emigrated to the Low Countries, whence, having established congregations there, they organized in 1620 the pioneer expedition to America, and began to return to England in the 1630s, when the power of Cromwell was clearly in the ascendant. The Dissent which was left in England was very largely Presbyterian, and during the reign of James I and the early years of Charles I it had short shrift from the Anglican Establishment. The mounting tension between the King and Parliament, which began in 1629 and ended in the King's execution twenty years later, provided a background for Cromwell's political and religious insurrection against the Establishment, and, although Cromwell himself favoured the Independent or Congregational churchmanship, the religious opinion that opposed Anglicanism was very largely led by Presbyterians. The Westminster Assembly of Divines was therefore Presbyterian as regards the affiliation of the majority of its members, and in its doctrinal ethos. In 1645 it was the clear conviction of those who held religious power that the Church of England must be no longer Episcopal but Presbyterian, and that it must be a Church united in principle with the Church of Scotland on the basis of the Solemn League and Covenant.

The document which emerged from the Assembly as a guide to faith and doctrine was the consequence of much heated discussion, and runs to the considerable length of some 14,000 words, in thirty-three chapters, each divided into many paragraphs. Its doctrine is Calvinistic in emphasis, much influenced by Knox's Confession and the Geneva Confessions. But its form is new, and it is not framed on the model of any existing Confession, being, so far as form goes, nearer to the Thirty-nine Articles than to any of the Reformed statements. But its ample language and combination of lucid theological statement with scriptural precision place it, as a statement of Reformed theology, far above any of the other Confessions in any language. It stands almost at the end of the period of classic Confessions, and forms a worthy climax to them. It is singularly free from truculent denunciations either of Rome or of heresies. It is more consistently positive in all its statements than any of its predecessors.

It differs from most other confessions especially in the space it gives to the interpretation of the doctrine of Scripture's authority (I 7-9), to the Covenant between God and man (VII), to Liberty of Conscience (XX) and to the manner of worship (XX). What is new in its teaching is the consequence of theological movements during the first half of the seventeenth century—especially of the Arminian Controversy. On the special matters which are our concern, its distinctive teaching is as follows.

Free Will. Free will, possessed by man in his state of innocence, was lost at the Fall (in the sense that he had then no free will to do good). On conversion, a man is freed from bondage to sin, but only by God's grace is he enabled to will freely what is good. The will of man 'is made perfectly and immutably free to good alone in the state of glory only' (IX).

Election ('Effectual Calling'). This calling is of God's grace alone, and those who receive it and respond to it are, with their children, 'the elect'. Those who profess any religion but the Christian cannot be saved (X).

Justification. Those who are effectually called are also justified by God. This is done 'not by infusing his righteousness into them, but by pardoning their sins, and by accounting and accepting their persons as righteous: not for any thing wrought in then, or done by them, but for Christ's sake alone, not by imputing faith itself, the act of believing, or any other evangelical obedience to them, as their righteousness, but by imputing the obedience and satisfaction of Christ unto them, they receiving and resting on his righteousness by faith; which faith they have not of themselves: it is the gift of God' (XI 1). Faith is alone the *instrument* of justification but is not alone in the person justified, being accompanied with all the other saving graces, and working by love (XI 2). (Cf. *The King's Book* on Faith, p. 100), above.

Each man is justified when the Holy Spirit applies Christ to him (§ 4); when justified, a man can never fall from the state of justification, but can fall under the Father's displeasure and require a forgiveness which, on profession of repentance, is always available (§ 5).

This chapter is followed by brief chapters on *Adoption* (XII), *Sanctification* (XIII) and *Saving Faith* (XIV), which is the gift of the Spirit, and whose principal acts are 'accepting, receiving and resting upon Christ himself for justification, sanctification and eternal life'. Of *Good Works* (XVI) it is declared that men may be moved to good works by God's Spirit, but (in agreement with the Thirty-nine Articles, XIV) there is no thought of a man's being able to do more than God requires. Only the regenerate can do good works which receive the approval of God, and these are approved not because of their own merit but because God 'looks upon them in his Son' (XVI 6-7).

The elect (or the 'Saints') are commanded to persevere and must guard against the assaults of the devil which may bring them to the displeasure of God (XVIII), but justified men may claim an assurance of justification on the ground that once justified they are never utterly cast away (XVIII). True believers are not without obligation to the Law of Christ (XIX —against Antinomian views), but they live in liberty of Conscience—that is, they are able to use their free will to please God so far as in this world it is possible to please him (cf. IX above). But a claim to freedom of conscience can never rightly be advanced as an excuse for sin (XX).

The Church (XXV-XXVI). The universal Church is invisible and consists of the whole number of the elect; the visible Church is also universal, and is the kingdom or family of God, outside which there is no ordinary possibility of salvation (XXV 1-2). The catholic Church has been sometimes more, sometimes less visible (cf. Calvin *Inst.* IV 1, 2: p. 111 above). depending on the purity of local Churches (XXV 4-5). Christ alone is head of the Church (§ 6). The Communion of Saints (XXVI) is the unity which the elect have in Christ their common head. This does not imply community of goods, but community of service, edification and charity.

Church Discipline (XXX-XXXI). The Church retains the right of censure and admonition, for the purifying of the body (XXX). For the government of the Church synods and councils are appointed, and these should be called by the magistrate unless he is an open enemy of the Church, in which case synods may meet without him. Synods must not be regarded as having authority except where they follow the Word of God, and must deal only with strictly ecclesiastical matters (XXXI).

The Sacraments (XXVII). In every Sacrament there is a 'spiritual relation or sacramental union' between the sign and the thing signified. Their efficacy depends not on the piety or intention of him who administers it but upon the work of the Spirit and the word of institution. There are two Sacraments only.

Baptism, a rite of admission to the Church and a seal of the covenant of grace with all its implications (§ 1) may be administered by sprinkling (§ 3) and upon infants (§ 4). Grace and salvation are not 'inseparably annexed unto it' (§ 5), and its efficacy is once for all time (§§ 6-7).

The Lord's Supper (XXIX). Its purpose is 'the perpetual remembrance of the sacrifice of Christ in his death, the sealing of all benefits thereof unto true believers, their spiritual nourishment and growth in him, their further engagement in and to all duties which they owe unto him, and to be a bond and pledge of their communion with him and with each other as members of his mystical body' (XXIX 1).

The Sacrament is not a repetition of Christ's sacrifice (§ 2); communion in both kinds is to be given (§ 3), but only to those present in the congregation, private masses being forbidden (§ 4).

'The outward elements in this sacrament, duly set apart to the uses ordained by Christ, have such relation to him crucified, as that truly, yet sacramentally only, they are sometimes called by the name of the things they represent' (§ 5; cf. XXVII 2).

I

Transubstantiation is abhorrent to sense and faith (§ 6). Those who receive worthily, 'inwardly by faith and indeed, and yet not carnally and corporally but spiritually, receive and feed upon Christ crucified'. Christ is present, being 'not corporally or carnally in, with, or under the bread and wine', but 'spiritually present to faith' (§ 7). Those who receive unworthily may receive the outward sign but do not inwardly receive the thing signified (§ 8).

Church and State. The statement on a Christian man's duty to swear at the magistrate's bidding is an amplification of Article XXXIX in the Prayer Book (XXII). That on the Civil Magistrate (XXIII) states the normal Calvinist doctrine that the magistrate's business is to preserve the public good but not interfere with the ministry of the Word and Sacraments, that it is the Christian's duty to obey him, including making war (§ 2), and that the magistrate must take what steps are necessary to preserve order in the Church and prevent corruptions and suppress blasphemies (§ 3). Ecclesiastical persons are not exempt from his authority, even if he is an infidel; but the Pope has no power at all over the civil magistrates in England (§ 4).

The Westminster Confessions remains normative for the faith of the Church of Scotland and the Presbyterian Church of England. An important variation of it, however, is the statement of faith that was published by the Independents or Congregationalists, known as

THE SAVOY DECLARATION, 1658

This document was published towards the end of the Commonwealth, and its chief author was John Owen (1616-83). Independency, owing to the pre-eminent prestige of Cromwell, gained an ascendancy for a short period over Presbyterianism, and the revised document was published in order to correct (as the Independents saw it) certain emphases in the Westminster Confession with which they did not find themselves in agreement.

Towards the beginning of the Westminster Assembly, in 1644, five 'Dissenting Brethren' recorded their disagreement with the majority on the matter of Church government, believing that the Westminster Divines were over-clerical in their approach to this matter. The document they prepared was published as the *Apologeticall Narration*—in which the word 'Congregationalism' is for the first time used in its modern denominational sense. The nearness of the Independents to the theological position of the Presbyterians is attested by the fact that almost the whole of the Westminster Confession was accepted by them when they came to codify their belief. But at certain important points there are divergences.[1]

Savoy has thirty-two chapters against Westminster's thirty-three. Chapters 1 to 19 are the same in both; Savoy interpolates a new Chapter 20. S 21 to $30 = W$ XX-XXIX. S then omits W XXX and XXXI, and S 31-2 = W 32-3. After the Confession of Faith, S adds a 'Platform of Polity' stating the principles on which Churches of the Congregational Order are to be governed.[2]

Although there are large variations between S 7 and W VII, and S 15 and W XV (which latter chapter is wholly rewritten in S), the doctrinal content of both in both cases is the same. There is a tendency for S to prefer a more evangelical tone at some points: for example, in S 18, which may be compared with W XVIII, 'of Assurance'.

W § 2: 'This certainty is not a bare conjectural and probable persuasion, grounded upon a fallible hope, but an infallible assurance of faith, founded upon the divine truth of the promises of salvation, the inward evidences of those graces

---

[1] These can most conveniently be studied in A. G. Matthews, *The Savoy Declaration* (1958), which is a photographic reprint of the section in Williston Walker's *Creeds and Platforms of Congregationalism* (New York, 1893) that deals with the Declaration. All divergences are noted typographically, with the original readings in the footnotes. Matthews's edition, however, has an important modern introduction.

[2] A brief account of the Platform of Polity will be found in my book, *The Story of Congregationalism* (1962), and it is, of course, treated in full in Williston Walker and A. G. Matthews, *op. cit.*

unto which these promises are made, the testimony of the
Spirit of adoption witnessing with our spirits that we are the
children of God: which Spirit is the earnest of our inheritance,
whereby we are sealed to the day of redemption.'

S § 2: 'This certainty is not a bare conjectural and probable
persuasion, grounded upon a fallible hope, but an infallible
assurance of faith, founded on the blood and righteousness of
Christ, revealed in the Gospel, and also upon the inward
evidence of those graces unto which promises are made, and
on the immediate witness of the Spirit, testifying our Adoption,
and as a fruit thereof, leaving the heart more humble and holy.'

There is, at many points of small alteration, a tendency to
emphasize faith, even more than *W* does. For example, at
S 1 10 (= *W* I 10), the final words in *W* are: '. . . no other, but
the Holy Spirit speaking in the Scriptures', which in *S* are
rendered '. . . no other but the holy Scripture delivered by the
Spirit; into which Scripture so delivered, our Faith is finally
resolved'. Similarly, to the end of *W* II, *S* 2 (§ 3) adds the
words, 'Which Doctrine of the Trinity is the foundation of all our
Communion with God, and comfortable Dependence upon him.'

The interpolated Chapter 20 in *S* 'Of the Gospel, and of the
extent of the Grace thereof', is, as is explained in the Preface
to the Confession, deemed to be a logical and necessary
interpolation after *W*'s article on 'The Law of God', which is
substantially repeated at *S* 19. The substance of the chapter
is the theology of the Holy Spirit which was the special
contribution of the English theological puritans to Christian
thought. (It is to be found, for example, in John Owen's
Pneumatologia and Thomas Goodwin's *Of the Work of the Holy
Spirit in our Regeneration*.) Its insertion, while it adds nothing
substantial which could not in general terms be deduced from
W, marks *S* with a special 'English Puritan' ethos which gives
it a touch of uniqueness at this point. In summary, it teaches
that the promise of Christ to the Elect leads to Faith and
Repentance, and the Gospel revealed in this promise is effectual
for the conversion of sinners (§ 1). This promise is revealed only
in the Word of God; the works of Creation and Providence,

and the light of nature, are all insufficient to 'make discovery of Christ'. The revelation is a function of God's free grace, and that it may be given to all nations, God has ordained the preaching of the Gospel. But 'although the Gospel be the only outward means of revealing Christ and saving Grace, and is as such abundantly sufficient thereto; yet that men who are dead in trespasses may be born again, quickened or regenerated, there is moreover necessary an effectual, irresistible work of the holy Ghost upon the whole soul, for the producing in them a new spiritual life, without which no other means are sufficient for their conversion unto God' (§ 4).

In Sacramental doctrine, *S* follows *W* with alterations only of detail (such as 'called' for 'ordained', of the qualification of a minister for dispensing the Sacraments, *S* 28 § 4; cf. *W* XXVII 4). But there is a significant dissent in respect of the Magistracy (*S* 24 = *W* XXIII).

W had laid it down that magistrates have authority to preserve the unity and peace of the Church by the suppression of blasphemies and heresies, and that to this end they have the right to call synods, be present at them, 'and provide that whatsoever is transacted in them be according to the mind of God'. *S* strongly disagrees, and puts it thus (we quote the whole of *S* 24 § 3):

'Although the Magistrate is bound to encourage, promote and protect the professor and profession of the Gospel, and to manage and order civil administrations in a due subserviency to the interest of Christ in the world, and to that end to take care that men of corrupt minds and conversations do not licentiously publish and divulge blasphemy and errors in their own nature, subverting the faith and inevitably destroying the souls of them that receive them:

'Yet in such differences about the Doctrines of the Gospel, or ways of worship of God, as may befall men exercising a good conscience, manifesting it in their conversation, and holding the foundation, not disturbing others in their ways of worship that differ from them; there is no warrant for the Magistrate under the Gospel to abridge them of their liberty.'

In other words: the magistrate must keep the peace and allow the Church to live in quietness in the world, but must be given no power to decide matters of doctrine or worship, or to force decisions concerning them. Since it was precisely at this point that the authors of S dissented from those of W is was important for them to make clear their repudiation of the magistrate's right of interference at these points. For according to W, the magistrate could call a synod and at once suppress the dissenting minority for their non-conformity to Presbyterianism.

A modified form of this, incorporating the dissent against the magistrate's power to call synods, was included in the Massachusetts Confession (Boston) of 1680; but this put the first half of the declaration more strongly: 'They who upon pretense of Christian liberty shall oppose any lawful power, or the lawful exercises of it, resist the Ordinance of God, and for their publishing of such opinions . . . may be lawfully called to account.'[1] The latter half of the paragraph they left as it stands in S.

The American Presbyterians altered W at this point in 1788, to include the decisive sentences, 'No law of any commonwealth should interfere with, let or hinder the due exercise thereof [*sc.* of the government of Christ in his Church] among the voluntary members of any denomination of Christians, according to their own profession of belief.' It further forbade any exercise of violence, abuse, injury or indignity on the magistrate's part on the persons of those who fell under their discipline.

On the Church, S 26 §§ 2 and 5 make considerable alteration of W XXV 2-7. S § 2 omits the phrase 'out of which there is no ordinary possibility of salvation' in its rewritten version, and where W in §§ 3-4, declares that the catholic Church is given the ministry, oracles and ordinances of God for the gathering and perfecting of the saints', S § 2 insists that while the catholic Church is the 'whole body of men throughout the world professing the faith of the Gospel', this is the *visible* Church,

[1] See Walker, *op. cit.*, pp. 393 f.; Matthews *op. cit.*, pp. 108 f.

and as such it is not 'intrusted with the administration of any ordinances', nor has it any officers to govern or rule over the whole Church. It also omits the statement in W § 4 that the Church is sometimes more, sometimes less visible. The denial of ecumenical authority to the visible universal Church, and of its right to appoint ecumenical officers, was a Brownist touch in S which remains peculiar to classic Independency, and which of course has passed out of modern Independent thinking.

S § 5 corresponds to nothing in W, but being a rhetorical expression of confidence in the triumph of the true Church over Antichrist, adds nothing of moment to doctrine.

The Preface to S explains[1] that its authors have taken some care to omit from the Confession what is proper to a manual of discipline, and that it is for this reason that certain passages are omitted from W. Manuals of discipline are outside the scope of the present study, but it may here just be said that the 'Platform of Polity' which follows the Confession of Faith in S expounds the polity of Independency, and to some extent illustrates the special contentions underlying S's explicit modifications of W noted above. It is there made clear (§ 6) that there are particular Churches whose government is self-sufficient, and 'besides these particular Churches there is not instituted by Christ any Church more extensive or Catholic entrusted with power for the administration of the ordinances or the execution of any authority in his name'. That illustrates chapter 26 of the Confession. In § 26 of the Platform it is, however, stated that where there are differences of doctrine or matters of administration, the proper body to settle them is an *ad hoc* synod of the neighbouring Churches. These synods have no 'church power', but by their help and advice the mind of Christ is to be sought in such emergencies.

THE CAMBRIDGE PLATFORM, 1648

Contemporary with these two English documents is the very important American statement of church polity, *The Platform*

[1] Page xxi of the original edition (1658); Walker, *op. cit.*, p. 363.

of Church Discipline (Cambridge, Massachusetts, 1648). The only doctrine with which it is concerned is that of the Church, but in its seventeen chapters it goes more thoroughly into this than any similar English-speaking document. Although it is a manual of discipline, it falls under our review because it is wholly concerned with a doctrine. It was the outcome of a Synod held at Cambridge to determine the life and manners of the newly-founded Congregational Churches of the Pilgrim Fathers in the New World. Briefly, this is what it says:

The Catholic Church is the whole company of those that are elected and redeemed and in time effectually called to salvation (II 1). The Church is Triumphant (in heaven) and Militant (on earth), and the Church Militant is both visible and invisible: visible, in respect of the open profession of the Christian faith and its gathering in particular churches, invisible in its relation to Christ, 'as a body unto the head, being united to him by the spirit of God and faith of their hearts' (II 3-4).

There is no universal-visible Church. Church discipline applies to members of the Church visible and militant, and these members walk together in congregational Churches. National or tribal Churches are of the old covenant; congregational Churches, of the new. A congregational Church is a part of the Church militant and visible, consisting of 'a company of saints by calling, united in one body, by a holy covenant, for the public worship of God and the mutual edification of one another in the fellowship of the Lord Jesus'. (The term 'independent' is rejected, § 5, for reasons which appear later.)

Chapter III says that the Church consists of informed and responsible Christians and their children, and that no Church should be larger in membership than can conveniently meet together, or smaller than can duly carry on Church work. Such Churches are formed on the basis of a Covenant of agreement (IV); Covenant is a better basis of membership than private faith, a formal profession of faith, 'cohabitation' (i.e. living near one another: the parish system) or (by itself) Baptism. Covenant, responsible agreement with Christ and with one another, must be added (IV 5). Power in each Church belongs to its own elders and to nobody outside it (V). The officers of a Church are Pastors, Teachers, Ruling Elders and Deacons (VI-VII) and they are elected freely by their fellowships (VIII). Ordination of all Church officers is to follow their election, and to be conducted by the laying on of hands (IX).

The Government of the Church (X) is 'in prespect of the headship of Christ, a monarchy, in respect of the brotherhood of believers, a democracy, in respect of the power of the Presbytery (i.e. officers) an aristocracy'. All power is of Christ; the power of the officers is to guide and lead, that of the brotherhood to choose its officers, admit members, and edify one another.

Chapters XI to XIV deal with the maintenance of officers of the Church (including the payment of ministers), the admission of members, the removal of members from church to church, and excommunication; all these involve issues with which the spiritual power of the brotherhood must learn to deal.

Chapter XV deals with the important matter of the Communion of Churches, enjoining on separate churches the necessity of caring for one another, consulting one another, admonishing one another and sharing in one another's worship at the Lord's Table. Churches are encouraged to propagate, founding new fellowships where the original one has become over-large.

Of Synods, Chapter XVI says that when necessary the Churches should exercise their right to call them, for consultation on doctrine and discipline. The magistrate may call a synod to advise him in matters of religion (§ 3), provided it is understood that a synod is an act of the Church and not of the civil power.

The Magistrate (XVII) holds power to which Church power is not opposed, and which must be used for the furtherance of the Church's concerns, and not for their restraint. No magistrate may compel anybody to join the Church (§ 4). Church officers should not 'meddle with the sword of the Magistrate' (§ 5), nor the magistrate with work proper to Church officers. But the magistrate must restrain idolatry, blasphemy and heresy, and (§ 9) 'if any church . . . shall grow schismaticall, rending itself from the communion of other churches or shall walk incorrigibly or obstinately in any corrupt way of their own, contrary to the rule of the word; in such case the Magistrate is to put forth his coercive power, as the matter shall require'.

The Cambridge Platform expounds the Congregational doctrine of the Church more completely than any other English speaking document, and it is of especial importance in that it seeks to lay down a polity for no dissenting minority, but for a Church whose universal hold over a whole country (as they then saw it) was more confidently to be hoped for than any Church which could have been founded at Savoy. Congregationalism of this doctrinal and mildly federal sort became the Establishment in New England. The Platform was printed in 1648, and by 1651 enough replies from Churches had been received at the General Court at Boston for that Court to seal the document as the rule of Church life throughout Massachusetts. This it remained, with legal sanction, until 1780. To a large extent its authority prevailed also in the colonies of Plymouth, Connecticut, and New Haven.

IX.—THE FAILURE OF THE HEADS OF AGREEMENT, 1691

LOOKING back over the Confessions that have so far come under review, the reader cannot fail to observe in their succession a certain pattern comparable to that of a ship lurching through a heavy sea with a shifting cargo. First one, then another theological point is brought into prominence, and all the others are gathered round it. Broadly speaking, in the Lutheran tradition all doctrines are aligned with the special doctrine of *faith* which is held in the Lutheran Confessions. In the Calvinistic documents, it is Election, a consequence of the special doctrine of God's sovereignty, which conditions the expression of all the other doctrines.

To be truly stated, therefore, the doctrines which they hold in common with other Christians have to be stated by the Confessional Churches in terms conformable with their special doctrinal insights. This has consequences which are not usually foreseen by the authors of the Confessions, and which contain unexpected dangers. The chief danger could be described as a condition of 'unstable equilibrium' in the communion which issues the Confession. The urgent contentions of the Confession tend to be understood, and lived up to, and faithfully held, only when the communion which issues it is, as it were, 'on the move'. The heat of the controversies that occupied the years 1530-1661 in Europe was enough to keep the communions engaged in them conscious of their special doctrines and their special contribution to the preservation of the Faith. Yet even here, the history of the Lutheran Communion shows that by 1600 the Augsburg Confession was hardly being regarded as a living document; and the horrors of the Thirty Years' War (1618-48) brought that communion not to a revival of the faith of Augsburg so much as to the new evangelical zeal of pietism.

In pietism there was much more of the Anabaptist ethos than Luther or Melanchthon would have tolerated in the Churches of their day.

It must be conceded that on the whole Confessions tend to have a low survival-value as incitements to faith and church-manship. The most evident exception to this is the Westminster Confession, which, with its Catechism, has remained a living force in the Church of Scotland to this day. This cannot be separated from the fact that W is by far the most competent and catholic piece of theological writing in the literature of the Confessions. But of the others it is fair to say that to some extent they are all dead letters now, so far as the living faith of their communions is concerned. Even the Thirty-nine Articles, which continue to be printed in all editions of the Book of Common Prayer, are a document from which the ongoing faith of the twentieth-century Church of England could hardly be inferred; their denunciations of all things Papal are quietly ignored in many parts of the Church of England, and their doctrines are seldom preached as they express them.

The Calvinist Declarations and the Savoy Declaration have all been relegated in our time to the status of documents which are regarded by the present-day heirs of their concerns with more historical affection than present respect. The reason for this is quite simple: that Confessions are always in danger of petrifaction. Creeds, being fashioned out of theology, are at their best always able to make large allowance for the circumstantial differences between one age and that which preceded it: the proof of this is the manner in which (as our last chapter will show) Churches of the ecumenical age are tending to accept as they stand the 'Nicene' and 'Apostles'' Creeds, and to concentrate in their manifestoes on practical matters which are admitted to be strictly related to the present situation and not to imply basic theological dissents from the Creeds.

But Confessions fashioned out of temporal dissents, even though they profess to be the Confessions of national and even universal Churches, have always this serious disadvantage, that they do not allow for those 'growing points' which appear in the natural development of Christian church life. For example: the emergence of Lutheran monasteries in recent times is a matter which Lutherans have not been able to condemn, but which the Augsburg Confession would have frowned on. There is nothing in the French or Belgic Confessions which allows for such developments as the Protestant Community at Taizé. The Thirty-nine Articles expressly denounce the doctrine implied in the service of Benediction, which is held in not a few Anglican parish churches at the present time. The Savoy Declaration makes no provision for the order of Moderator, which appeared in 1919 in the Congregational Churches of England and Wales. None at all of the classic Confessions give any guidance which is helpful in two situations characteristic of the modern age—the situation of new indigenous Churches in foreign lands, and that of the lapsed and formal Christian at home. It is being found in practice that while no venture or innovation which commends itself clearly to the present age as a point of growth involves anybody in the refutation of anything in the 'Nicene' Creed, every such venture could be found to be forbidden at some point by a Confession: and in consequence, of course, opposition is always raised against such ventures by those who take their stand upon a Confession. (The Protestant Truth Society can quote the Articles: the conservative Dissenter can quote Savoy against Moderators: the literal adherence to the doctrine of Election makes it difficult for a Christian of that view to take much interest in missionary work—or, not to put it quite so boldly—it offers what appears to be an adequate excuse for him to withhold his interest from it.)

The affair of the 'Happy Union' and the 'Heads of Agreement', which took place in England in 1691, illustrates the dangerous inflexibility of Confessions, and the way in which those who followed them found themselves unprepared for a new historical demand.

From the beginning of the Commonwealth, the Presbyterian and Congregational Dissents in England were two separate bodies of opinion, and the frontier between them was clearly drawn in the *Apologeticall Narration*, and later in the *Savoy Declaration*. They differed, as we have seen, on points of church government and of evangelical emphasis. They differed not at all in their hostility to the Anglican Establishment.

Their respective Confessions provided—at Westminster— for a national Presbyterian Church, and —at Savoy—for a nation-wide (but not national) Church on the Congregational pattern. By a singular historical accident, persecution descended on both bodies within a few years of the publication of the second of these Confessions. Under that persecution the Presbyterians suffered the more heavily, because they were the larger body, but it was the Congregational pattern of church-manship which was proved and tested—for under persecution the independent and Congregational way is what any Church is temporarily obliged to follow. Central authority of any kind depends on communication, and where this breaks down, Churches must take their own line for the time being.

Nothing then could have been more natural than for the Congregationalists and Presbyterians, on the cessation of persecution, to look toward one another and examine at once the possibility of working together without disrespect to one another's consciences. This is what took place in 1691.

But even for this there was a precedent. Before ever the Savoy Declaration was published, in fact in the year 1656, the ministers of both persuasions in Cumberland and Westmorland published an Agreement which, while stating their differences, stated also that there was a large area of common ground. 'When we can neither agree in principle nor in practice,' they said, 'we are to bear with one another's differences,' but 'in the exercise of Discipline, it is not only the most safe course, but also the most conducing to brotherly union, that particular churches carry on as much of their work with joint and mutual assistance as they can with conveniency and edification'. Furthermore, 'although we differ as to the power of the associated churches over particular congregations; yet we agree that it is not only lawful and useful, but in many cases necessary, that several churches should hold communion and correspondency together.'[1]

There cannot have been many churches of both persuasions in Cumberland and Westmorland in 1656. The whole document reads very reasonably and prudently to the modern eye. But the gesture of 1691 was more impressive in its inception, being projected by 'the United Ministers in and about London, formerly called Presbyterian and Congregational' in the document called *Heads of Agreement*. In this document the right of churches to be self-governing is conceded (I § 1), but the necessity of synods for 'communion and correspondency' is pressed at many points (esp. I 6). It is stated that the rule of faith can be taken from the Confessions of either Westminster or Savoy (I 9).[2]

This was described as the 'Happy Union', and in its achievement one of the decisive influences was that of Increase Mather, a member of the Massachusetts Church at Boston, who was at the time acting as agent in England for the colony. He seems to have acted as adviser to the leaders of the two denominations (Matthew Mead, Congregationalist, and John Howe, Presbyterian), and to have infected them with his enthusiasm for unity through compromise. Mather was, of course, a son of the *Cambridge Platform*, and none could have better put the case that Congregationalism liberally interpreted was a rational and workable church polity. They had found this out in America in forty years of peace such as had been denied to their English cousins.

The effect of the Agreement in America was almost immediate. In the Saybrook Platform (1708) modifications were made to the Cambridge Platform which suggest a less exclusively Congregationalist approach to the polity of the expanding American Church. A liberal opinion which found *Cambridge* a shade over-doctrinaire in its exclusion of one local church from the influence of another was heartily pleased by the example that had been set in England.

[1] Williston Walker, *Creeds and Platforms*, pp. 453-4.
[2] *Ibid.*, pp. 455-462.

But the 'Happy Union' which was proclaimed on the publication of the *Heads* was short-lived. Within three years it was dead. The union which was founded on expediency and prudence was exploded by a theological controversy. The controversy itself hardly concerns us, except for the curious fact which its pattern brings to our attention. These briefly are the facts: one Mr. Crisp, the son of Dr. Tobias Crisp (d. 1643), began to draw further attention to the theological teaching of Crisp senior just about the time of the 'Happy Union'. Crisp senior was an anglican clergyman whose opinions had at the time been widely condemned as antinomian.[1]

These opinions, on their second publication, drew some support from nonconformists, but were violently attacked by Dr. Daniel Williams, a Presbyterian minister (the same Dr. Williams who founded the famous library, schools and other benefactions). Although the Congregationalists of London did not particularly favour Crisp's teaching, they dissented from Williams's attack, and took occasion (here we see the cloven hoof) to note that Dr. Williams was one of the Presbyterians who were 'most filled with a prejudiced spirit against the Government of the Congregational Churches'. In the dispute which followed Crisp was virtually forgotten: but the Congregationalists claimed to be ranged on the side of liberty of the spirit, and that the Presbyterians were the apostles of legalism; to the Presbyterians the Congregationalists appeared obstinately to favour a disorder and contempt for theological precision for which Presbyterianism must always stand.

Now this is worth analysing. It could be put thus: that while there is one major direction in which *S* differs from *W*, and of which the parties to the 'Happy Union' were fully conscious, there is another difference which they overlooked. That to which they attended, and over which they sought reconciliation, was the matter of Church Government. That which they overlooked was a temperamental opposition to legalism which

---

[1] Among these opinions were 'that Jesus Christ became for our sakes not only human but a sinner, and that the true believer could achieve a holiness which was the same as that of Christ'.

Congregationalism always felt, but rarely expressed with precision, vis-à-vis the Presbyterians. This expresses itself in *S* at many places which might well be overlooked by a contemporary reader who was not assiduous in his attention, and are usually indicated by an expansion of evangelical reference, or of reference to the work of the Holy Spirit, in *S*.[1]

What matters is to notice that the difference between *S* and *W* on Church Government (see above, pp. 124-127) is fully present to the minds of the parties to the 'Happy Union', while clearly the difference of theological emphasis is only half-consciously present. The result of this second fact is the Congregationalists' apparent defence of a doctrine in Crisp which they did not really approve, and their taking occasion to attack at once the character and theology of a contemporary Presbyterian, with whom they were supposed to be living in harmony.

The passage from the age of Confession to the age of Ecumenicity could not be more aptly illustrated. This is always the kind of difficulty that arises. That which is explicit in the Confession is not the whole of the Confession's influence on its adherents. In later times we have tended to distinguish between 'theological' and 'non-theological' factors in the obstacles to church unity. The history of the confessions indicates that it might be well better to distinguish between 'primary confessional' and 'secondary confessional' factors. The 'Happy Union' was founded in reconciliation over primary confessional factors; it was upset by the emergence of secondary confessional factors which had not been considered in the negotiations for reconciliation. The historical consequence was unmitigated disaster for English Dissent, in that the Congregationalists found themselves inadequately defended against a disorderly evangelicalism, and the Presbyterians were vulnerable to an over-intellectual dogmatic legalism that sent many of their

[1] The reader will, of course, easily identify these variations in A. G. Matthews's edition (1958) of *Savoy*. He is especially invited to consider such passages as chapter 15, wholly rewritten in *S*, and the *S* modifications in XI 1, 3; XVII 3; XVIII 2 and XX (rewritten).

K

most distinguished ministers and congregations into the error of Unitarianism. The tendency in the eighteenth century to gloss over the exacting problems of church order produced problems in foreign missionary work which have brought the third and fourth generation of missionary promoters into grave difficulties.

It is for this reason that, as we shall see, the ecumenical movement has been non-confessional, but rather a movement based on adherence to creeds and the seeking of practical reconciliations. It will be seen further that the doctrine around which our problems now gather is that of Episcopacy, but that those who take the most responsible part in discussions of it do so with a full knowledge of the danger of gathering *doctrines* around the problem-centre. This they have learnt from the examination of the perplexities into which the Confessions brought those who sought to live by them.

X.—MODERN CONFESSIONS AND CONTROVERSIES

WE now pass to the modern period of the Ecumenical activity of the divided Church, in which two great documents have been produced which will primarily occupy our attention—the Statement of Faith upon which the Church of South India is now doctrinally based, and the Basis of Union of the United Church of Canada.

Some apology must clearly be given for the abrupt transition from the year 1700 to the year 1920. And some comment must be offered on the difference between the situations prevailing at those two dates.

First, it can fairly be said that the age of the great Confessions ends in Europe with the Confession of Westminster, and in America with the Cambridge Platform and its modifications up to 1708. (The Cambridge Platform is the first and also the last American classical statement.) But what do we mean by a 'classical' statement? We mean a statement of faith made on the assumption that the Church which makes it is, or will come to be, a world-wide (or at least a nation-wide) Church. That, and nothing less, is the assumption of the Reformed Statements. These all reject the Church of Rome as a Church outside the covenant of grace; and while a measure of toleration must be supposed between the traditions of Luther and of Calvin on the continent of Europe, all the Confessions of both traditions speak of 'the Church' as an invisible company of believers who are in the sight of God separated from the infidels but who form a Church which is not limited by national boundaries. The English and Scottish Confessions speak for bodies which are to be the Churches of their countries. The Savoy Declaration speaks for a body which was really believed to be the coming Church of England. Westminster, both by incorporating so much of the Thirty-nine Articles and by repudiating so

much else, was regarded by its compilers as a perfectly workable substitute for those Articles. The assumption was that the
Church of England would now be Presbyterian: and the
assumption of John Owen at Savoy was that it would be
Congregational.

The doctrine of Election satisfactorily disposed of the
unbelievers. Whether it confined its scope to the believers, or
whether it went on to state the predestination of all unbelievers
to perdition (whether or not they appeared to be 'in the Church'
at any given time), it assumed that the believers were here
and the unbelievers there, even if the dividing line between
them was known only to God.

What never occurred to the formulators of the Confessions,
and never could have occurred to them, is the situation of an
'unchristened' Europe and America—a world in which the vast
majority of people were in a condition, not of ignorance, but of
residual Christianity. This situation, upon which all modern
Christian comment is based, and to which all Western Christians now admit that they are heirs, is that in which hardly
anybody holds a full Christian faith or acts on it, in which a
very small proportion of the people of the nations under
review profess the faith by attending church, in which, of those
who do attend church or profess the faith, only a small minority
have any theological consciousness at all, and in which it is no
longer necessary to guard the Church against the intervention
of the magistrate because the great majority of magistrates will
not waste their time by attending, in either a friendly or a
hostile spirit, to the affairs of the Church.

This is a profound change of climate and atmosphere.
Consider its effect on two of the great beliefs which we have
especially considered—Election and the doctrine of the Church.
Today it is so clear that residual Christianity informs a majority
of minds, while the Christianity which the Confessions proclaim
informs virtually none (apart from those of professional
ministers), that the distinction between 'believer' and 'un-
believer' becomes altogether irrelevant to modern thinking. It
is probably only a minority among professing Christians who

seriously think nowadays that Christianity is confined to those who believe in the inerrancy of the Bible and the final judgment upon all those who do not make conventional profession of their faith. (Though the formidable increase in the membership of fundamentalist groups and sects insists that we limit the judgment to 'probably'.)

On the other hand, there remains in many countries a notion that one can be formally attached to the Church without having any open or personal Christian profession at all. Many anglican clergy hold that all souls living within a parish are theirs to care for, whether or not they make Christian profession (and in the case of some, even if their profession is made by allegiance to the Roman Catholic Church or to a Free Church). In the Scandinavian countries it is assumed, except open profession be made to the contrary, that every member of the nation is a member of the Church; and we are told that in these countries the relation of nominal to openly professing Christians is almost 100 to 1.

Consider the following words from the opening chapter of Doddridge's *Rise and Progress of Religion in the Soul* (1740):

'Religion, in its most general view, is such a sense of God on the soul, and such a conviction of our obligations to him, and of our dependence upon him, as shall engage us to make it our great care to conduct ourselves in a manner which we have reason to believe will be pleasing to him. Now, when we have given this plain account of religion, it is by no means necessary that we should search among the savages of the African or American nations, to find instances of those who are strangers to it. When we view the conduct of the generality of people at home, in a Christian and Protestant nation, in a nation whose obligations to God have been singular, almost beyond those of any other people under heaven, will any one presume to say, that religion has a universal reign among us? Will any one suppose that it prevails in every life; that it reigns in every heart? Alas! the avowed infidelity, the profanation of the name and day of God, the drunkenness, the lewdness, the injustice, the falsehood, the pride, the prodigality, the base selfishness, the stupid insensibility about the spiritual and eternal interests of themselves and others, which so generally appear among us, loudly proclaim the contrary. So that one would imagine, upon this view, that thousands and tens of thousands thought the neglect, and even the contempt of religion, a glory rather than a reproach. And where is the neighbourhood, where is the society, where is the happy family, consisting of any considerable number, in which, on a more exact examination, we find reason to say, "Religion fills even this little circle"?'

That is the kind of sentiment which, suitably translated, might adorn the front page of any modern paper-backed book of apologetic; but in 1740 it sounded a new note—the note, indeed, which was about to be sounded more universally and evangelically by John Wesley. Doddridge's *Rise and Progress* is one of the first 'popular books on religion' in English; it is deliberately written simply and for a wide audience (its author says so in his Preface), and it is deliberately written on the assumption that religion is already receding from what was supposed to be a Christian country.

It is no coincidence that Doddridge was also one of the first English Protestants (and perhaps the first English non-Anglican) to show a practical and intense interest in foreign missions. He expresses this constantly in his hymns and his preaching. Much that he wrote and said is uttered as to a society which again needs a corporate conversion, and not as to a society which may be assumed to hold the Faith and needs only such exhortation as will deepen an already existing understanding of it.

The subsequent history of religion in England is not confessional but very largely social. The great difference between Wesley's revival and Luther's Protest was the inseparable social circumstances and emphases of the former. Similarly their after-effects are distinguishable. In the eighteenth century Wesley drew the attention of Christians to the need of an unevangelized mass of people in the lowest classes of society. In the nineteenth people who had come under his influence (though it might be at several removes) drew their atttention to the needs created by the Industrial Revolution. The vital principle in English religion became active, rather than contemplative and dogmatic, and even the Oxford Movement is gravely misunderstood if it be thought of as merely a gesture of domestic reform (or counter-reform) in the Church of England. There is no important movement of thought—in discipline, dogma, Biblical criticism or ecumenical activity— which in the days following 1700 is not to some extent conditioned by a consciousness of the need that the Gospel be communicated to those who have not heard it, at home and abroad. Therefore the old controversies are realigned. On the one hand there is a new kind of controversy—between the claims of religion and those of science, for example: on the other, there is a growing conviction that the divisions between the communions are not ultimate, and are an impediment to the Church's evangelistic purpose.

Social developments assisted the ecumenical developments at home—the greater mobility of the ordinary Christian, the opening of the universities to Dissenters, the increasing opportunities for personal encounter between people, and classes of people, who formerly were not encouraged to mix. Moreover, the fact that history was remorselessly demanding that the Christian communions render account for their former complacency, and suffer the assaults of a secularism which none but a pious fanatic was able to call wholly evil, caused Christians to turn their attention away from the cherished doctrine of Election (which to many seemed to be the ground of that complacency for which they were now paying), and towards the doctrine of the Ecumenical Church.

THE UNITED CHURCH OF CANADA

Of modern Confessions, the nearest in form to the older pattern is that contained in the *Basis of Union* of the United Church of Canada (1924).[1] This is, of course, only a modest

[1] Bell, *Documents on Christian Unity*, I 65 (pp. 232-8).

gesture of ecumenicity, in as much as the uniting Churches were all of what in England would be called the Free Church pattern; they were Presbyterian, Congregational and Methodist communions only. Controversy therefore lay very largely in the field of Church Government, and the only doctrinal controversy there may have been is between what remains of Calvinism in the Presbyterian and Congregational Churches, and of Arminianism in the Methodist.

The section on Doctrine in the *Basis of Union* is set out in twenty brief articles, running to not more than 2,000 words. The expression of doctrine in these is broad rather than precise, and there is none of that trenchancy which is characteristic of the Confessions of the sixteenth and seventeenth centuries. Articles V and VI, *Of the Sin of Man* and *Of the Grace of God*, show the style adequately. .

V. 'We believe that our first parents, being tempted, chose evil, and so fell away from God and came under the power of sin, the penalty of which is eternal death; and that, by reason of this disobedience, all men are born with a sinful nature, that we have broken God's law, and that no man can be saved but by his grace.'

VI. 'We believe that God, out of his great love for the world, has given his only-begotten Son to be the Saviour of sinners, and in the Gospel freely offers his all-sufficient salvation to all men. We believe also that God, in his own good pleasure, gave to his Son a people, an innumerable multitude, chosen in Christ unto holiness, service and salvation.'

The word 'chosen' is the only reference to the doctrine of Election in the statement. But the doctrine of the Church is further elaborated in XV:

XV. 'We acknowledge one holy Catholic Church, the innumerable company of saints of every age and nation, who being united by the Holy Spirit to Christ their Head are one body in him, and have communion with their Lord and with one another. Further, we receive it as the will of Christ that his Church on earth should exist as a visible and sacred brotherhood, consisting of those who profess faith in Jesus Christ and obedience to him, together with their children, and other baptized children, and organized for the confession of his name, for the public worship of God, for the administration of the Sacraments, for the upbuilding of the saints, and for the universal propagation of the Gospel; and we acknowledge as a part, more or less pure, of this universal brotherhood, every particular church throughout the world which professes this faith in Jesus Christ and obedience to him as divine Lord and Saviour.'

Concerning the Sacraments, the Confession says (XVI 1) that the proper subjects of baptism are believers and believers' children, and that (XVI 2) the Lord's Supper is a 'sacrament of communion with Christ' in which the people receive it in faith 'do, after a spiritual manner, partake of the body and blood of the Lord Jesus Christ'.

The United Church of Canada is Presbyterian in government and very largely in ethos. Its *Hymnary* (1930)[1] is strongly influenced by Scottish practice but differs from the *Church Hymnary* (1927) of Scotland in a heightened evangelical emphasis which was clearly gained from the non-Presbyterian Churches in the Union. But its Confession is as uncontroversial and unexclusive as a Confession can well be. It makes no reference to the errors of others, and leaves room for a wide interpretation of its carefully worded statements. In the succeeding sections of the *Basis of Union*, the polity of the United Church is worked out, but again not by way of defending this polity against such others as episcopacy, but rather by way of producing a workable basis of church practice. The Episcopal Church in Canada and the Baptists took no part in the Union, so that the document stands as a good example of a partial union that avoids all the most dangerous points of modern controversy.

---

[1] There is a case for saying that the hymn books of the modern denominations are a better source for a judgment of their confession and belief than the documents they publish. This is an accidental but not unimportant factor in the modern confessional situation.

THE CHURCH OF SOUTH INDIA

The most impressive piece of ecumenical wrestling of our time is, of course, that which issued in the formation of the Church of South India. This Church, basing its belief on the classic Creeds, does not stand upon a Confession of its own; but the stages by which it came into being produced evidences of high controversy, and of important gestures towards reconciliation.

The South India United Church, a federation of Presbyterian and Congregational Missions, was formed in 1908 by the members of the London Missionary Society, the American Board of Commissioners for Foreign Missions, the Church of Scotland, the United Free Church of Scotland and the Dutch Reformed Church in America. At a later stage these were joined by the congregations of the Basel Mission. This was the first step towards a united Church of South India.

In May 1919 ministers of the South India United Church met with clergy of the Anglican Church (in all, thirty-three), and issued a statement from Tranquebar, South India, that proved to be of historic importance.[1] The basis of the statement is in the words from its second paragraph: 'We believe that the union is the will of God, even as our Lord prayed that we might be one, that the world might believe.' At once the statement proceeds to the controverted ground, and says that the united Church must contain these three scriptural elements: the *Congregational*, by which every member has immediate access to God, 'each exercising his gift for the development of the whole body'; the *Presbyterian*, 'whereby the Church could unite in a General Assembly, Synods or Councils in organized unity', and the *Episcopal*, which should be 'representative and executive'.

Concerning this last, the anglican members 'stand for the one ultimate principle of the *historic Episcopate*. They ask the acceptance of the fact of Episcopacy, and not any theory as to its character.' The members of the S.I.U.C. asked that the

[1] Bell, *op. cit.*, I 71 (pp. 278-81).

Episcopate 'reassume a constitutional form', and that in it 'spiritual equality' be recognized between all believers.

Union was therefore proposed on the 'common ground of the historic Episcopate and spiritual equality of all members of the two Churches', and on the basis of the Scriptures, the Apostles' and Nicene Creeds, and the two Sacraments of Christ's institution. It was repeated that 'the acceptance of the fact of the Episcopate does not involve the acceptance of any theory of the origin of Episcopacy nor any doctrinal interpretation of the fact'.

Episcopacy, then, is the centre of controversy. The mission field was the place in which it could be appropriately shown how far the denominations had travelled from the position taken up in the 'Free Churches' from the days of Martin Marprelate and his tracts (1588-9) to those of Thomas Binney, who in the mid-nineteenth century called the national Church in England 'a great disaster'. Episcopacy was in this new context a matter of controversy, but no longer of irrational hatred. Working from the Tranquebar statement, then, the representatives of the Anglican Synod of India and Ceylon defined 'constitutional Episcopacy' in March 1920[1] as requiring (a) that bishops be elected by representatives of the diocese and approved by representatives of the province; (b) that the bishops perform their duties in accordance with such customs of the Church as shall be defined in a written constitution, and (c) that continuity with the historic Episcopate be effectively maintained, it being understood that no particular interpretation of the historic Episcopate be demanded. All future ordinations were to be performed by the laying on of hands by bishops and presbyters of the united Church.

The first ten years saw energetic developments in this project. In March 1929 a Joint Committee of the Church of India, Burma and Ceylon, the South India United Church, and the South India Provincial Synod of the Wesleyan Methodist Church approved a Scheme of Union which gathered up and elaborated all the points in the original draft of 1919

[1] Bell, *op. cit.*, I 75 (p. 289).

including that concerning the interpretation of the historic Episcopate.[1] But although in the development of the Union, 'questions of faith caused no prolonged difficulties',[2] its movers declined to make haste. It was wisely decided to leave a period of thirty years for the uniting Churches to learn to live together, and for the formulation of doubts and dissents. Of these by far the most important were those which came from the head-quarters of the Anglican Communion at Lambeth.

THE CONTROVERSY CONCERNING EPISCOPACY

For the reasons for this we must briefly rehearse the history of that Lambeth Conference which has in our own country become the focal point of ecumenical thinking.

The first Lambeth Conference was called in 1867 by Arch-bishop Longley, for the discussion of domestic affairs; but twenty-one years later the Conference of 1888 first showed signs of its ecumenical future. At that Conference a report was received and affirmed which had originated in the United States, and which contained the original form of a document that proved to be historic. Two years before (1886) the General Convention of the Protestant Episcopal Church in the U.S.A., meeting in Chicago, had stated:

'We do hereby affirm that the Christian unity now so earnestly desired . . . can be restored only by the return of all Christian Communions to the principles of unity exemplified by the undivided Catholic Church during the first ages of its existence which principles we believe to be the substantial deposit of Christian Faith and Order committed by Christ and his Apostles to the Church . . .

'As inherent parts of this sacred deposit, and therefore as essential to the restoration of unity among the divided branches of Christendom, we account the following, to wit:

1. The Holy Scriptures of the Old and New Testaments, as the revealed Word of God.

[1] Bell, *op. cit.*, II 139 (pp. 143-191).
[2] Rouse and Neill, *History of the Ecumenical Movement* (1953), p. 474.

2. The Nicene Creed as the sufficient statement of the Christian Faith.
3. The two Sacraments—Baptism and the Supper of the Lord—ministered with unfailing use of Christ's words of institution and of the elements ordained by him.
4. The historic Episcopate, locally adapted in the methods of its administration to the varying needs of the nations and peoples called of God into the unity of his Church.'[1]

That is the statement of faith which is now known as the 'Lambeth Quadrilateral', or more precisely as the 'Chicago-Lambeth Quadrilateral'. As accepted by the Lambeth Conference of 1888 the statement suffered certain verbal changes, the chief of which was the addition of the 'Apostles' Creed' to clause 2. The statement has been reaffirmed by all later Lambeth Conferences.

But at the Conference of 1920[2] the statement was included, with a new emphasis in 'An Appeal to all Christian People'. In its sixth paragraph the first three clauses were quoted as a basis of unity, but instead of the fourth it was stated in § 6 that 'a ministry, acknowledged by every part of the Church as possessing the inward call of the Spirit, but also the commission of Christ and the authority of the whole body' is an indispensable factor of unity, and then in § 7 it is asked, 'May we not reasonably claim that the Episcopate is the one means of providing such a ministry?' And then it proceeds thus: 'It is not that we call in question for a moment the spiritual reality of the ministries of those Communions which do not possess the Episcopate. On the contrary we thankfully acknowledge that these ministries have been manifestly blessed and owned by the Holy Spirit as effective means of grace.'

---

[1] This was the first public and confessional form of this statement. But its origin is in a book published by William Reed Huntington in 1870, *The Church Idea—An Essay Toward Unity*, which was designed to promote Church unity in America, and which contained these four points stated in almost exactly this form. See Rouse and Neill, *op. cit.*, pp. 250 f. and 264 f.

[2] Bell, *op. cit.*, I 1 (pp. 1-5).

On this note the conversations towards the uniting of the Protestant Churches in Britain were officially opened (although the influence of the first Edinburgh Conference of Faith and Order, 1910, upon the spirit of this Conference cannot be exaggerated).

Once again, and in parallel to the Indian situation, questions of faith—that is, the first three of the four points of the Quadrilateral—have occasioned little difficulty. It is the Episcopate (and the consequent doctrine of the ministry) that always provides the stumbling-block. But the Lambeth Appeal of 1920 was received, and in most places warmly received, by the English Free Churches,[1] and the progress of the later developments can be traced in the four volumes of Bishop Bell's *Documents on Christian Unity*.

This emergence of the Episcopate as a point of living controversy, upon which the Church of England was prepared to reason with the non-episcopal communions, produced a situation of anomaly between the Church of England and the developing Church of South India which was concisely expressed in the Report of the Committee of the Church of England on the Unity of the Church, presented to the Lambeth Conference of 1930. The authors of that report[2] were obliged to point out that 'the Anglican Communion will . . . be in communion with the united Church, which will itself be in communion with bodies not in communion with the Anglican Communion'. It was therefore necessary for that Conference to judge in its Encyclical Letter that 'the united Church in India will not itself be an Anglican church', and for William Temple in 1944, in a letter to the Metropolitan of the Church of India, Burma and Ceylon,[3] to state in his capacity as Archbishop of Canterbury the limitations which would lie upon non-episcopally-ordained presbyters in the united Church vis-à-vis the Churches of the Anglican Communion. He stated there that while no censure would attach to a communicant

---

[1] Bell, *op. cit.*, I 30-41 (pp. 104-169), and II 118-131 (pp. 68-114).
[2] Bell, *op. cit.*, III 147 (p. 15).
[3] Bell, *op. cit.*, III 205 (pp. 225-8).

of the Anglican Communion who presented himself at the altars of the united Church in India, a non-episcopally ordained presbyter would have no rights of priesthood on an Anglican Church.

That situation remains since the foundation on 27 September 1947 of the Church of South India. It exposes the weakness which was necessarily left in its constitution by the 'saving clause' concerning the historic Episcopate.

A SKETCH OF A UNITED CHURCH, 1936

The only English document which attempted to break through the perplexity left by the acceptance of an Episcopate without prescription of any particular interpretation of it was *A Sketch of a United Church,* published from Lambeth Palace with a foreword by the then Archbishop of Canterbury (Cosmo Lang) in 1936. This was the report of a Commission consisting of thirty-eight ministers and clergy, equally divided between the Church of England and the Free Churches, in accordance with a resolution of the 1930 Lambeth Conference.[1]

In 'sketching' a constitution of a united Church, this commission repeated what had been said in India—that Congregational, Presbyterian and Episcopal elements were to be expected in any united Church. On the specific question of Episcopacy, however, they said this:

'The agreement formerly reached, that episcopal ordination in practice should be generally accepted, was subject to the understanding that such acceptance "would not imply the acceptance of any particular theory as to its origin or character". Experience has shown that this phrase raises certain difficulties of interpretation. Accordingly it seems better to say that in agreeing to include the Episcopate, together with the Presbyteral and Congregational elements of Church order, we also agree that the constitution of the united Church must leave room for, and recognise as permissible, various theories of the origin and nature of the Episcopate.' (§ 20).

The authors of *A Sketch* then proceed to distinguish the two

[1] Resolution 44 of 1930. Bell, *op. cit.,* III 145 (p. 6).

theories of Episcopate as (1) that which holds that the Bishops were appointed by Apostles, or men whom the Apostles had appointed, and (2) that which holds that the Episcopate emerged from the Presbyterate. The first view obliges its holder to the consequential view that Episcopacy is necessary to the Church, the second leaves its holder free to say that the Church can, under the Holy Spirit's guidance, modify its constitution (since the emergence of Bishops from Presbytery constitutes in itself such a modification); but the authors of *A Sketch* then go on to say that union should not wait for the resolution of this difficult problem (here for the first time officially brought out into the open), but that room must be left in the united Church for either of these views. They imply that no other view of the Episcopate is serious enough to be considered, and they had already said clearly (§ 18) that the secular authority must have no control over the spiritual actions of the Church councils, court or assemblies. The appointment of bishops by the Crown (a practice against which Free Churchmen have always manifested a lively conscience) is thus implicitly rejected.

The *Sketch* was followed in 1938 by an *Outline of a Reunion Scheme for the Church of England and the Free Churches in England*.[1] This provided for an episcopally organized Church with a General Assembly, Diocesan Synods, and local Congregational Councils (these last formed from within each local church). It was suggested that there need not necessarily be only one bishop in each diocese, and that an ex-Anglican and an ex-Free Church bishop might well share the duties (or where necessary, more than these two, drawn from both traditions) (IX 1). It was also stated that 'the acceptance of episcopal ordination for the future would not imply the disowning of past ministeries of Word and Sacrament otherwise received. . . . It would allow for various theories regarding the origin and character of the Episcopate. It would imply the continuity of the Episcopate of the united Church with the historic Episcopate in its succession from ancient times. It

[1] Bell, *op. cit.*, III 175 (pp. 71-101).

neither affirms nor excludes the view that Apostolic Succession determines the validity of the Ministry and Sacraments' (V 5). The Episcopate, indeed, was to be regarded as merely the most natural expression of the truth that 'no man can take this ministry upon himself' (V 2). But this did not commend itself as it stood to the Free Churches, who offered criticisms based on their claims to retain in any united Church the principles of evangelical freedom, and on the implications of the Lambeth Appeal's (1920) being addressed not to 'churches' but to 'communions' (was this to deny the status of 'churches' to the Free Churches?)[1]

There were very real difficulties, also, concerning the principle in the Free Churches that the ordained state was not necessary for a man (or in some, a woman) to administer the Sacrament of the Lord's Supper; and the Congregationalists were troubled about the exclusion from the proposed united Church of the non-sacramental Christians of the Salvation Army and the Society of Friends. Finally, the Free Churches stated that they were unwilling to be involved in a union which would further divide them from any with whom they were at present in Communion. The matter therefore rested at that point until conversations were reopened after the Second World War.

CHURCH RELATIONS IN ENGLAND, 1950

In that great complex of ecumenical conversations, then, which includes the growth of the Church of South India and the progress of relations between the Church of England and the Free Churches in Britain, Episcopacy has been the point around which controversy has continued to gather. From end to end of these colloquies and documents we find no discussion —or at least no disagreement—on transubstantiation, on predestination, on baptism, or even (this one point apart) on the nature of the Church. The pattern repeated itself in the Lambeth Conversations of 1948-50, in which discussion between the Church of England and the Free Churches was,

---

[1] Bell, *op. cit.*, III 177 (pp. 101-119).

L

through its representatives, renewed. In consequence of the Cambridge Sermon delivered by the then Archbishop of Canterbury (Geoffrey Fisher)[1] the conversations were gathered round the special point, whether the Free Churches could, as a step towards reunion, 'take Episcopacy into their systems'. In the Report published at the end of the conversation under the title *Church Relations in England* (1950), it was stated that there was no disagreement on doctrine at any point. 'All acknowledge', they said, 'the apostolic faith as contained in the Scriptures and expressed in the Apostles' and Nicene Creeds'.[2] But the point concerning Episcopacy was one to which the Free Churches could not at that stage give a clearly friendly reply.[3] The unusual complexity which the parties to the Conversations recognized in the English situation involved the Free Churches in traditional loyalties which have not yet been reconciled with the demands of unity. It remains therefore that the Free Churches remain divided from the Anglicans on the question of the historic Episcopate, and in consequence they cannot yet meet at one another's altars.[4]

Further comment is beside the point in a record of confessional developments. It remains only to note that the present century differs from all others since the Reformation in being an age in which the unity of Christian Churches is regarded as more to be desired than the clear statement of their differences. The old Confessions stated differences. In our time dogmatic Confession is taken for granted, and specific points of difference are being attacked with the object of reconciliation. Confessional documents are therefore few, and records of conversations many, various and extended. Theology is invoked as a reconciling factor, not as a divisive factor. But what remains unwritten—and this is what really distinguishes the present age from all the others—is the profound change in the spiritual

---

[1] For the relevant passage, see Bell, *op. cit.*, IV 236 (pp. 47-50).

[3] Bell, *op. cit.*, IV 237 (pp. 50-61; esp. p. 58).

[2] Bell, *op. cit.*, IV 238 (Baptists), 239 (Methodists) (pp. 61-74).

[4] For a discerning and lucid comment by a Protestant on Episcopacy, the reader should consult chapter III of Daniel Jenkins' *The Protestant Ministry* (1958).

climate, both without and within. The South India Scheme
and the Lambeth Appeal both begin from the same ground:
that in our age the Church cannot afford any longer to be
disunited, and that union in the will of Christ is an urgent
necessity if the Church is to survive the assaults of secularism.
This is not how they spoke in the sixteenth century. Corres-
pondingly there has developed within the Church a climate in
which the parties to discussions assume that they may speak
with what Bishop Stephen Neill (a prominent figure in the
later stages of the South India developments) was the first
to call 'brutal frankness', and that this will lead to a deepening
of a sense of mutual need. Meanwhile, the World Council of
Churches (which held its first plenary sessions at Amsterdam
in August 1948) has continued to work towards the widening
of the fields in which the communions may work together,
especially in works of mercy.

Although the Malines Conversations of 1924 between
Anglicans and Roman Catholics[1] proved virtually abortive,
other events of world-history, less spiritual in character, have
played their part in producing new relations between Protestants and Catholics. In this sense, perhaps the late Adolf Hitler
played the part of 'Cyrus, my servant', in being responsible for
a world upheaval in the midst of which Christians could no
longer ignore one another or contend with one another. It is
not only, indeed not primarily, theological developments that
have resulted in a visit (1960) of Geoffrey Fisher, then Archbishop of Canterbury, to Pope John XXIII, and a projected
(though, at the time of writing, widely disputed) visit to the
same destination of the Moderator of the Church of Scotland.

[1] See Bell, *op. cit.*, I 90 (pp. 338-349).

BIBLIOGRAPHICAL NOTE

The Confessions of the Reformed Churches may be consulted in the following sources.

P. Schaff, *The Creeds of the Evangelical Protestant Churches* and *History of the Creeds of Christendom* (both published by Hodder & Stoughton in 1877). *CEPC* contains the texts, *HCC* the commentary, as follows:

Augsburg: CEPC, pp. 1-73 (Latin and English); HCC, pp. 225-244.

Formula of Concord: CEPC, pp. 93-180 (Latin and English); HCC pp. 258-340.

Second Helvetic: CEPC, pp. 233-306 (Latin); HCC, pp. 390-420.

French: CEPC, pp. 356-382 (French and English); HCC, pp. 490-501.

Belgic: CEPC, pp. 383-436 (French and English): HCC, pp. 502-508.

Canons of Dort: CEPC, pp. 550-558 (Latin); HCC, pp. 519-523.

Thirty-nine Articles: CEPC, pp. 486-516 (English: editions of 1563 and 1571, with American Revision of 1801); HCC, pp. 615-653.

Scottish Confession: CEPC, pp. 437-479 (Old Scots and Latin); HCC, pp. 680-685.

Westminster Confession: CEPC, pp. 600-673 (English and Latin); HCC, pp. 753-782.

Savoy Declaration: CEPC, pp. 707-729; HCC, pp. 832-833.

Schaff is now difficult to obtain outside the more comprehensive libraries, although it remains the most complete compendium of Creeds and Confessions. It does not contain the *Cambridge Platform* nor the *Canons of the Council of Trent*.

B. J. Kidd's *Documents of the Continental Reformation* (Oxford, 1911) has the following selection:

Augsburg: Latin text only, pp. 259-288.

French: French text only, selection, pp. 668-673.

Belgic: Brief selection from French text, pp. 685-686.

Scottish Confession: Scottish text, selection, pp. 704-707.

H. Bettenson's *Documents of the Christian Church* (Oxford, World's Classics, 1943) contains the following selection (always in English):

Augsburg: Selection, pp. 294-298.

Westminster: Selection, pp. 344-348.

Council of Trent: Selection, pp. 365-373.

Other sources for the material discussed in this book are these:

Augsburg and the *Formula of Concord.* On the theology of Martin Luther, see E. G. Rupp, *The Righteousness of God* (1953); P. S. Watson, *Let God be God!* (1947); the two volumes of translations by B. Lee-Woolf, *The Reformation Writings of Martin Luther* (1952, 1956); and for a modern approach in an ecumenical setting, Flew and Davies, *The Catholicity of Protestantism* (1950), a pamphlet emerging from the Lambeth Conversations of 1948-50, especially pp. 67-90.

Calvin, Calvinism and the Institutes. See the new translation of the *Institutes* in the S.C.M. Press Library of Christian Classics, vols. XX and XXI (1961), with its introduction and notes. Also A. Dakin, *Calvinism* (Duckworth, Studies in Theology, 1940).

Scottish Confession. This is included in John Knox's *History of the Reformation of Religion in Scotland*, of which several editions exist (e.g. ed. Lennox, Melrose (London), 1905). For a study of the Scottish Catechisms and their Calvinist origins, see T. F. Torrance, *The School of Faith* (1958).

Westminster Confession. See W. M. Hetherington, *History of the Westminster Assembly of Divines* (Edinburgh, 1878); A. F. Mitchell and J. Struthers (ed.), *Minutes of the*

Westminster Assembly, 1643-9 (Edinburgh, 1874); S. W. Carruthers, *The Daily Work of the Westminster Assembly* (Philadelphia and London, Presbyterian Historical Societies, 1943); S. W. Carruthers, *Three Centuries of the Westminster Confession* (Fredericton, N.B., 1957). See also next entry.

Savoy Declaration. See Williston Walker, *Creeds and Platforms of Congregationalism* (New York, Scribner, 1893) pp. 340-408. The full text of pp. 368-402 has been reprinted photographically in A. G. Matthews (ed.), *The Savoy Declaration, 1658* (London, 1958), together with the full text of the Platform of Polity and an Introduction. In Walker (and therefore also in Matthews) the variations between *S* and *W* are printed in heavy type, and the originals of *W* in footnotes. The book therefore forms a complete text of both Confessions.

The Cambridge Platform. Williston Walker, *op. cit.*, pp. 194-237 (full text and commentary).

The Council of Trent is most handily to be studied in B. J. Kidd, *The Counter-Reformation*, 1550-1600 (1933), pp. 53-113.

The documents of the modern ecumenical movement are collected in the four volumes of G. K. A. Bell, *Documents on Christian Unity* (Oxford University Press, 1924, 1930, 1948, 1957). Pamphlets and occasional papers in this context are too numerous to mention here. The reader should especially consult Rouse and Neill, *History of the Ecumenical Movement* (1953) and the documents published by the World Council of Churches from its first general Assembly at Amsterdam (1948): *The Universal Church in God's Design, The Church's Witness to God's Design, The Church and the Disorder of Society, The Church and the International Disorder* (all published in 1948), and W. A. Visser 't Hooft (ed.) *The First Assembly of the World Council of Churches* (1949). *A Sketch of a United Church*, published in 1936 by S.P.C.K. is at the time of writing (1961) out of print.

INDEX OF DOCTRINES